revolutionary voices

A Multicultural Queer Youth Anthology

revolutionary voices

edited by

amy sonnie

Manufactured in the United States of America.
Printed on acid-free paper.

This trade paperback original is published by Alyson Publications,
P.O. Box 4371, Los Angeles, CA 90078-4371.
Distribution in the United Kingdom by Turnaround Publisher Services Ltd.,
Unit 3 Olympia Trading Estate, Coburg Road, Wood Green,
London N22 6TZ England.

First edition: October 2000

01 02 03 04 10 9 8 7 6 5 4 3 2

ISBN: 1-55583-558-9

Credits
• "America's on Sale!" by Alix Lindsey Olson first appeared in *Only the Starving Favor Peace*, Feed the Fire Press, Sept. 1999.
• "Beginning Revolutions" by Colleen Donovan appeared in *Capitol Q News*, May 1997 and *Seattle Gay News*, May 1997.
• "Dancing in the Shadows" by Siobhan Brooks first appeared in *Trikone* magazine, Vol. 13, No. 3, July 1998.
• "exorcisms" by sts first appeared in the 'zine *nightmare girl #2*, Oct. 1996.
• "grown-up" by Ahimsa Timoteo Bodhrán first appeared in *Vital Signs*, Vol. 1, Issue 2, April 1998.
• "illustrations" by sts first appeared in the 'zine *Way Down Low*, 1998.
• *Impossible Body* has appeared in *The Journal of Lesbian Studies* and *The Lesbian Polyamory Reader*, ed. Marcia Munson and Judith P. Stelboum, Haworth Press, 1999.
• "Line" by Sherisse Alvarez first appeared in *Waterways* Chapbooks, 1997.
• "This is to me..." by Jason Roe first appeared in the 'zine *Kill the Robot* #6, 1995.
• "*was ich bin*" by Ahimsa Timoteo Bodhrán first appeared in *Expressions*, Jan. 1998.
• "Why Life?" by Cecilia Isaacs-Blundin first appeared in *Sojourner: The Women's Forum*, Oct. 1997.
• Cover design by B. Zinda.

contents

acknowledgments

I would like to thank my advisors Rosaria Champagne and Margaret Himley for supporting and enabling this project, for reading it time and again, and for helping me to recognize my own authority.

I am grateful to all of my friends and family for their support of this project, especially to my mother, Lynn, and father, Brian, and my sisters, Katie and Laura; to Liz Tenenbaum, Ivonne Mari Miranda, and Bree Zuckerman for helping me keep my sanity and being both friends and intellectual/creative inspiration; to Dani Montgomery, MC Ettinger, yk hong, Malachi Larrabee-Garza, Jaime Vines, Damon Azali, Adam Jernigan, Cheryl Dumesnil, and Kat Aaron for the additional help; to the Syracuse University Honors Program and Women's Studies Department; to Robin Riley, Karen Hall, Ahimsa Timoteo Bodhrán, Margot Kelley Rodriguez, Oriana Bolden, and Catharine Donahue for the feedback; Corin Tucker, Kathleen Hanna, and Nicole Demerin for the resources and recommendations; to Tammy Rae Carland, Pat Califia, Phoebe Hanshew, David Zucker, and Dan Woog for the correspondence; to Ken Carl and everyone at the National Youth Advocacy Coalition; to the coordinators of the Young, Loud, and Proud Queer Youth Conference and the wonderful students at Colgate University for allowing me to share this work in progress at the "Breaking Down Society's Closet" conference in March 1998.

Thank you as well to the numerous organizations, past and present, that have been an alternative to the mainstream and an inspiration to young queers committed to radical social and political transformation.

I would like to thank all those who have E-mailed or called over the past three years to share ideas, offer support, and ask when this collection would be finished. Your interest in the project has sustained my hope and motivation. Most importantly, I would like to acknowledge each and every one of the contributors to this anthology. This book would not have been possible without you. It is your talent, strength, and courage that has made the collection such an incredible resource. I would like to specially acknowledge the contributors whose works shaped this collection but for one reason or another are not included. I have grown so much from working with all of you, and am grateful for your willingness to share. You are my family, my community.

Speaking for Ourselves: A Note From the Editor

Thank you for picking up *Revolutionary Voices*, a creative resource collection *by* and *for* queer[1] and questioning youth. A first-of-its-kind anthology, this book was created as a forum for today's queer youth movement to address the issues that shape our lives.

As youth who have "grown up" during the '80s and '90s, we are the product of a unique historic moment in which queer youth are increasingly visible and coming out at younger and younger ages. These days many of us have greater access to community and support. From gay-straight alliances to LGBT centers, from media visibility to the Internet, queer youth are finding and creating community all over the globe. Increased visibility, however, also means an increase in the attacks against us. And with youth coming out in larger numbers and from more disparate communities, it is all the more urgent that we talk about how our identities as young queers intersect with our cultural, racial, and economic backgrounds.

Revolutionary Voices attempts to open up this dialogue for youth: to move beyond coming-out testimonials and recognize the process we go through in questioning, understanding, and *re*questioning our identities as queers. Whether exploring gender or racial identity, eating disorders or organized religion, substance abuse or mental health, each contributor wrestles in some way with how the intersections of race, class, gender, sexuality, religion, age, and ability impact our lives.

We have unique stories to tell, and distinct cultures and experiences to communicate. We have something to say about how our world is run and who runs it. And in a world that constantly tries to speak for us, this book asserts that we are our own experts. That *we* can speak for ourselves.

Countering the Silence

I started this project in 1995, when I was 19, to create a venue for young queers to discuss the questions we are facing and the issues we are passionate about. I envisioned the project as a 'zine, hoping to find grants to fund distribution and production. In 1996 I began circulating calls for submissions (through flyers, letters, E-mail, word of mouth), and over the next year I grew even more convinced of the need for a book in which we could respond to the world around us.

All around me I saw that marginalized communities were under attack. In 1996 conservative politicians waged war on affirmative action; its abolition in California led to a 50% decrease in the enrollment of students of color in the state's top universities by 1997. This was also the year almost every major city in the United States welcomed the antigay, antifeminist Promise Keepers with open arms and money bags. This was the year I met Krista Absalom and learned that being gang raped while unconscious is not considered rape in New York State. This was the year I first heard about Brandon Teena, a 21-year-old who was brutally raped and murdered for being transgendered. Across the country young queers continued to take their own lives, young women starved themselves for a Kate Moss figure, and the United States continued to build more prisons than schools. Our communities were being pitted against one another. And we were failing to see the connections between these attacks, and further, our responsibility to act as allies to one another. As young queers from divergent backgrounds, we lacked a space and a common language with which to understand one another's stories.

And it did not stop in 1996. Over the past four years I have met and worked with queer youth from all over the world, and by all accounts, the attacks have increased. Some have even made headlines. Matthew Shepard has become a queer community icon, his murder a cornerstone in legislation against hate crimes in the United States. But why was his the only story about hate violence to dominate the news that year? Why was there no significant media coverage about the murders of trans queers of color such as Marsha P. Johnson or Tyra Hunter? Why no media martyrdom for James Byrd Jr., a black, differently abled man in Texas whose body was dragged behind a truck by three white men? Why does the bombing of a gay bar in London make international news, while violent attacks against queers and queer organizations in Zimbabwe receive no mention?

These are the politics of the world we live in—under a system that dictates whose lives matter and whose don't. Presenting the work of more than 50 individuals, *Revolutionary Voices* retaliates against these mandates. We speak to counter the silencing imposed on us; we speak to break the silence we have internalized. It was with this in mind that I sought a publisher who could help distribute this collection as widely as possible. We have created a family here. And standing in solidarity, we say, "We matter. Our *survival* is news too."

Who Are We?

From its inception to the published collection you have in your hands, the youth involved in creating this book have become a community, one that continues to inspire and nourish me. The contributors come from the United States, Puerto Rico, Canada, the Middle East, Europe, Asia, the Pacific Islands, Africa, and the First Nations of North America. They range in age from 14 to 26 and come from diverse ethnic, racial, social, and economic backgrounds. Many of these brave writers and artists are sharing their work for the first time.

Because so much published material simply reflects the status quo, *Revolutionary Voices* represents a conscious commitment to overrepresentational politics. I have deliberately created a collection that prioritizes the voices of the traditionally underrepresented: young women, transgender and bisexual youth, youth of color and mixed-blood youth[2], differently abled youth, and youth from low-income backgrounds.[3]

Still, this collection could be even more overrepresentative. The voices of trans and differently abled youth are, by my standards, underrepresented here, in addition to youth of color, especially Native American and Southeast Asian youth, queers under 16, and those from outside the United States. But it must be understood that this anthology is a *starting point*. It is a challenge for us all to continue creating and diversifying the mediums from which we speak.

To create a forum that reflects divergent as well as common histories, *Revolutionary Voices* presents a multicultural, multigendered, multigenre cross section of today's queer youth movement.

By **multicultural**, I mean: This collection includes the voices of youth from a variety of ethnic, racial, religious, economic, artistic, political, and gendered cultures. This is not a "melting pot" approach to multiculturalism, which erases individualities and tokenizes certain voices. We speak for ourselves, as ourselves, and recognize that more work is needed so that the nuances of our individual experiences are understood.

By **multigendered**, I mean: Many of us challenge traditional gender roles and assumptions that our assigned sex (male/female) must inform our gender (masculine/feminine). There are not only two sexes and two genders. Our lived experiences tell us otherwise. Some of the artists and writers in this book speak as FTM (female-to-male), MTF (male-to-female), trans-identified, gender-benders, fence-sitters, tranny girls, tranny boys, or something else entirely. This book is not just about the voices of gay and lesbian youth. It is about the voices of *queer* youth: gay, lesbian, bisexual, transgender, intersexed, questioning, and many others. In being multigendered, we advocate an end to a strict sex and gender system.

By **multigenre**, I mean: What you'll find within are not just diverse identities but diverse styles of communicating those identities. This collection includes poetry, interviews, essays, prose, performance pieces, sculptures, paintings, letters, diary entries, etchings, and collages in an effort to legitimate the many creative forms we use to express and represent ourselves. For this reason as well, the contributors' bios appear next to their writing or art. We see these as equally important pieces of writing in which we give both ourselves and our work a context.

Revolutionary Voices honors the artistry in all the things we have to say and all the ways we find to say them.

Language Lessons

Unlike previously published works focused on queer youth, *Revolutionary Voices* is written and edited *by* youth *for* youth, not by an adult who analyzes and filters our experiences for us. Though these collections are also important, it is necessary for us to claim the autonomy to represent ourselves.

Claiming this authority over our own experiences is particularly critical for us as youth because so often we are not taken seriously. Parents and teachers, peers and society tell us we are in a "phase," that we will "grow out of it." We are seen as works-in-progress, underdeveloped. Or, as queer Chicana poet Gloria Anzaldúa writes about her sisters of color, "The ability to respond is what is meant by responsibility, yet our cultures take away our ability to act—shackle us in the name of protection."[4] The same can be said about us as young people.

Part of the problem is that we have accepted this devaluation. From suicide to substance abuse, from apathy to violence within our own communities, the hatred we internalize is one of the most threatening and universal constants in our lives. Shame and self-hatred wound us, dividing us from ourselves and one another. This is precisely why we must find ways to strengthen and build our community, so that none of us are isolated, so that we discourage all forms of discrimination, so we learn to take care of one another, and continue to brave the elements of our own lives.

Revolutionary Voices has provided an alternative to self-abuse, a chance to use art and writing as a means of self-healing, self-exploration, and resistance. The pieces themselves are arranged to reflect this journey: from questioning to understanding, self-acceptance to resistance.

The pieces, as well, demonstrate that art and writing are mediums for truth, rawness, and honesty. They are the sites where we are often most real *and* most vulnerable—in our journals, in our sketchbooks, in our dialogues with each other. These are the spaces where we overcome silence and self-doubt, where we sketch out representations of ourselves and our reactions to the world around us. For this reason, *Revolutionary Voices* foregrounds *creative* work.

Creative work is political; words and images move people and have the capacity to dislodge deeply entrenched systems, if we arm ourselves with a voice and surround ourselves with allies. Writing and art are radical, especially when *what* we produce, *why* we produce, takes on the politics of necessity. We write about what we need, what we've fought for, how we're surviving, and the obstacles in our path. Our creative work is the starting place where we entreat larger social change, the place where we develop a radical consciousness—a revolution of words, ideas, and self.

This artistic expression takes many forms, but for a generation that has grown up on the spoken word and image—with hip hop, punk rock, MTV, digital culture, 'zines, and slam poetry—it's not surprising that many of us feel compelled to express ourselves with rhyme, rhythm, image, and a pen. Neither is it surprising that I received more poetry and spoken word submissions than any other genre. These are forms we can call our own. In many respects, they have become a common language we share. A language that tells *our* truths.

What's So Revolutionary About These Voices?

The young writers in this collection, like so many revolutionary thinkers of the past and present, are moving toward a radical consciousness by questioning heteronormativity and positioning themselves as young and queer in a world that tells us queerness and teen sexuality are discrepant. We think critically about regimes of gender, race, class, ability, and age.

We see that we live under a system of heterosexism, white supremacy, misogyny, and capitalism—where homophobia is wielded as a weapon of sexism; where most of us are taught a Eurocentric version of history in school; where young people, especially young people of color and poor people, are being tracked into prisons. This is a system that justifies spending more money on the military than on education and health care combined; a system where foreign business interests control peoples and nations of color and the United States bombs and sanctions whoever it pleases. This system makes possible a society that packages queer identities with rainbow ribbons and sells them to the highest bidder. A society in which Pride has been commodified.

We see that this is a system that privileges some of us at the expense of others—a world where we learn to hate and fear difference, but where we must relearn love of ourselves and of each other. And we are committed to challenging that system.

Unlearning mainstream society's teachings is a difficult process requiring visible alternatives and open dialogue. This collection is our attempt at opening this dialogue. We share our work to counter our own invisibility, to become allies to one another, and to demonstrate that we believe in ourselves enough to take up a pen, a paintbrush, or a camera in our own defense.

As a resource collection, *Revolutionary Voices* models some of the ways we defend ourselves and stand together in solidarity. It includes youth at different places in challenging and unlearning the deadly ideologies we have been taught. It allows us to teach and learn from one another. It demonstrates that prioritizing the voices of the underrepresented and speaking out as young people in a world that says we should be spoken for is a revolutionary act. This type of revolution begins in the heart. And in making heartfelt connections with others, we are able to build a consciousness with a holistic vision of social change.

In building this community, the contributors to this collection have inspired each other. Some have even begun editing other first-of-a-kind anthologies—by trans youth, by "crip queers," by queer mixed-bloods. We hope to inspire you as well. Whether you write a poem or start a gay–straight alliance in your school; whether you get involved in antiracist education or volunteer at a community center, we intend *Revolutionary Voices* to be a call to action for the creation of new, more diverse forums through which we can speak.

—Amy Sonnie
Fall 2000

Special thanks to the following for editing the editor: Tracy Bland, Ahimsa Timoteo Bodhrán, Oriana Bolden, Catharine Donahue, Colleen Donovan, Beth Ann Dowler, Qwo-Li Driskill, Alexia Exarchos, Damon Azali, Adam Jernigan, Carrie Katz, Emil Keliane, Erin Lathers, Sharon Martinas, Dani Montgomery, Salwa Nassar, Alix Olson, Margot Kelley Rodriguez, and Jaime Vines. I could not have finished this editor's note without your feedback, love, and affirmations.

[1] For the purposes of this preface, *queer* is used as an umbrella term for lesbian, gay, bisexual, and transgendered people. See the glossary for a more complete explanation of the term.

[2] The term *mixed-blood* refers to people who identify with their biracial or multiracial background. The term is not embraced by everyone of mixed descent. I use the term here, as distinct from people of color, to recognize the particular experiences and identities of mixed-race people in our society.

[3] Practicing respectful overrepresentation did not come without its challenges, and I did not navigate those challenges without a strong network of friends and mentors as well as a great deal of self-reflection. Ultimately, creating this forum for youth required establishing a relationship with every contributor, cultivating trust, and continuing to confront my own privileges.

[4] Anzaldúa, Gloria. *Borderlands/La Frontera: The New Mestiza.* California: Aunt Lute Books, 1987.

Introduction:
"We Are the Ones We Have Been Waiting For"[1]
Margot Kelley Rodriguez

When I first received an E-mail about *Revolutionary Voices* in 1997, it was a yet-to-be-named anthology by and for queer youth with an open call for submissions. I sent in my poetry, marking the start of a three-year collaboration and friendship that would reaffirm my faith in the revolutionary impact of art within the queer youth movement. I've been lucky enough to watch *Revolutionary Voices* evolve into an extraordinary collection that speaks out against the injustices in our communities, exposes the violence and pain we withstand, and celebrates our ability to survive in a world that quite literally does not want us. Writing the introduction to this book is both an honor and a responsibility. How do I give a project like this a context?

I can only speak from what I see, through the lens of a queer Chicana mixedblood who grew up in a racist world of violence and survived to become a warrior-poet. Homeless at 14, I slept in terror on San Diego beaches with one eye always open and one hand fisted around my father's stolen pocket knife. A year later I became a token in the LGBT movement, participating in the first-ever NGLTF Youth Leadership Institute, getting there by luck and hustling, only to find a world completely alien to me. At 16 I was arrested by the San Diego police under the guise of "curfew violation." I was booked and detained but knew I was lucky—this was my first altercation, while so many of my friends faced arrest and harassment daily. That same year I stood in front of my 11th grade English class and came out through an autobiographical presentation. As I was cross-examined and interrogated by my "peers," my teacher sat quietly in the back corner grading papers, and my twin brother hunched silently—so silently—in his seat, probably praying for the bell to ring. Yeah, I learned I couldn't depend on anybody, and I learned it pretty young, back when I was still a punk kid living on the streets. When shit flies, even blood cannot protect you. *¿Tu sabes?*

I do not know the particular geographies—the social localities—of each artist in this book. But their stories and essays, art and poetry evoke a familiar isolation and despair; the "I have nowhere to go" terror of hiding, of always running toward somewhere better. Now, more than ever, we find ourselves under attack—on the streets, on the news, on the state and federal level. The hatred and abuse of youth in this country grows with each hour. Look at our schools. We have outdated books, not enough chairs, no toilet paper. What we do have are brand-new, shiny metal detectors, plainclothes cops, security guards, and barbed-wire fences. Our schools have been war zones since way before the Columbine massacre. Recently the students I work with compared their high school to a jail. The gates are closed, they are in lockdown, the roaming security guards harass them whenever they leave their classrooms to go to the bathroom. If they question a teacher, they are sent to OCS—a kind of solitary confinement—sometimes for the whole day. On the adjacent corner, the city is building a new jail. The kids need to look no farther than across the street to see how the city is investing in their future.

It is not an accident that incarceration rates for young people, especially young people of color, have skyrocketed. The 1990s have become a decade of generational antagonisms fostered by fear and reinforced by media that sensationalizes the "horrific" instances of school and street violence. Meanwhile, the United States builds prisons instead of buying textbooks. In 1995 alone, our government built 150 new prisons and expanded 171 additional prisons. We spend billions of dollars locking up people to provide a new kind of "slave" labor instead of investing that money into our schools and our children's futures.

And though this might seem like rhetoric (books not bombs, teachers not cops), it's not. We are labeled predators but must walk through each day looking over our shoulders—fearing cops, doctors, and sometimes each other. Fenced in from birth, we are taught to take our anger out on ourselves, our own people, our peers, and our lovers. But what are our alternatives? The well-funded organizations, queer and otherwise, that should serve as a helping hand instead coerce us into silence. And some of us, those of us who are poor and of color, don't even get that far. We don't make it past the application process—except as the token Chicana, the token trannyboy.

In 1997 I helped organize the Youth Institute for NGLTF's Creating Change Conference. At every juncture the youth organizers were met with hostility, double-checked, and not trusted. We did not have a say in the agenda, we did not have a voice on the planning committee. Many of us never made it to the conference because the registration fee was so high. For those youth who did make it, we were expected to sit quietly on the sidelines, and if we voiced criticism we were made to feel "ungrateful" or "too radical."

The pressure to conform or "shut up" continues to alienate us to this day. We are not heard in the larger LGBT movement unless we play the part of passive victims, unless we look and act exactly like they do—proudly adorned with rainbow flags, working in co-opted nonprofits, lobbying for mere "tolerance," for more laws. Yes, we are coming out younger and in larger numbers. Yes, we can say there is a visible LGBT community; the "tolerance" and publicity generated by Budweiser-sponsored Pride parades gives us a face, a brand identity. But it is an old, white, conservative face—certainly not a face that represents us.

I am not saying that the mainstream movement is all just a bunch of shit. Historically it was once a grassroots movement that really paved the way for the last couple of generations to live with a little less fear. The drag queens and stone butches that took to the streets outside Stonewall Inn in 1969 were people of color and working-class queers. That night they fought against years of persecution and police harassment, against brutal beatings and repression that still happen every day in this country. They fought for dignity, not purchasing power. We started as a radical movement that fought against the state, but as the middle class took control, the movement's priorities shifted. All our resources moved to Washington, D.C., and the lobbying game began. We gained a language, we got national. We got tolerance (sort of), but we also got commodified, co-opted, and whitened. What was once a movement became an interest group.

As youth, we are here to shake things up, to call into question the mainstream's quest for legitimacy. We know that the face of oppression is like a chameleon, hiding itself in the very institutions that the mainstream LGBT movement seeks to join—whether through marriage or the military. We don't want to join the army; we want the military out of our neighborhoods and our schools. And why do we prioritize marriage when many of us still work the streets for a place to stay at night, when transgender folks are arrested and harassed by police, when the "justice" system turns a blind eye toward us? How can we work for laws when those who enforce the laws are the same people who terrorize us every night?

Revolutionary Voices serves as a wake-up call to our various communities, to the LGBT movement, to *Los Estados Unidos,* and to the world. These young artists shout out, "We have taken matters into our own hands, and we are mad as hell. We are here!" The mainstream movement calls us the "future." What the movement doesn't realize is that we are the *present*. We are not waiting for tomorrow, because we have something to say *right now*. And we have a vision that allows all of us to live in dignity without having to sacrifice any part of ourselves for one identity or another, for one community over another. We are not asking for an invitation to join the movement at the negotiating table. We are willing and determined to break that table.

We are part of a larger youth movement that truly deals with the multiple faces of oppression. We must, because we reflect those faces. We embody them all—as youth of color, as women, as the poor, the (dis)abled, and as queers. Youth span every community, from the queer kid in Nebraska to the young *mexicano* just up from Oaxaca. We are not tripping anymore, and yeah, we are pissed off and scared and tired—tired of running and fighting and struggling to survive, let alone change anything. But we must. We know our responsibilities to each other, and we know we've got to stick together, because this shit is real and we need each other now more than ever.

As artists, we come together in this book to share ourselves with each other and with you—from stories about coming out in junior high school to powerful declarations of self; from poems on love behind closed doors to spoken word pieces decrying the capitalist state of America. These artists paint the pained mutterings of heroin addicts and testify to the dehumanizing experience of mental ward cages. Included here are stories of loss (how religion can force a grandmother to turn her back on her granddaughter), stories of rage (against our parents, against hunger, against the state of things), and stories of love (about the awesome power of desire, about the beauty of touch). Throughout these testimonials runs a thread of hope; hope in love, hope that by writing this down we can help some other queer kid out there.

We know the answer to June Jordan's question, "Where is the love?"[2] The answer is us, "We are the ones we have been waiting for." We love against all odds. We get spit on, shot at, harassed, and abused, and still, still we love—even though it may cost us our lives.

Revolutionary Voices is a call to action. To all of you. To each and every individual who picks up this book. Because this is truth, raw and real and in your face. It may be harsh, but that is what truth is, and these artists have taken the leap to write it down. In a huge act of faith, we put it out into the world, not knowing whose hands it will end up in. But we did it anyway, to reach each other and to represent ourselves. We dedicate this book to us, to all of us, wherever we are; so we may continue to speak our minds and hearts, to struggle to save ourselves, and in doing so to save each other. It starts with us, so what are you waiting for?

[1] June Jordan, "Poem for South African Women," *Affirmative Acts: Political Essays*, 1998.

[2] June Jordan, "Where is the Love," 1978.

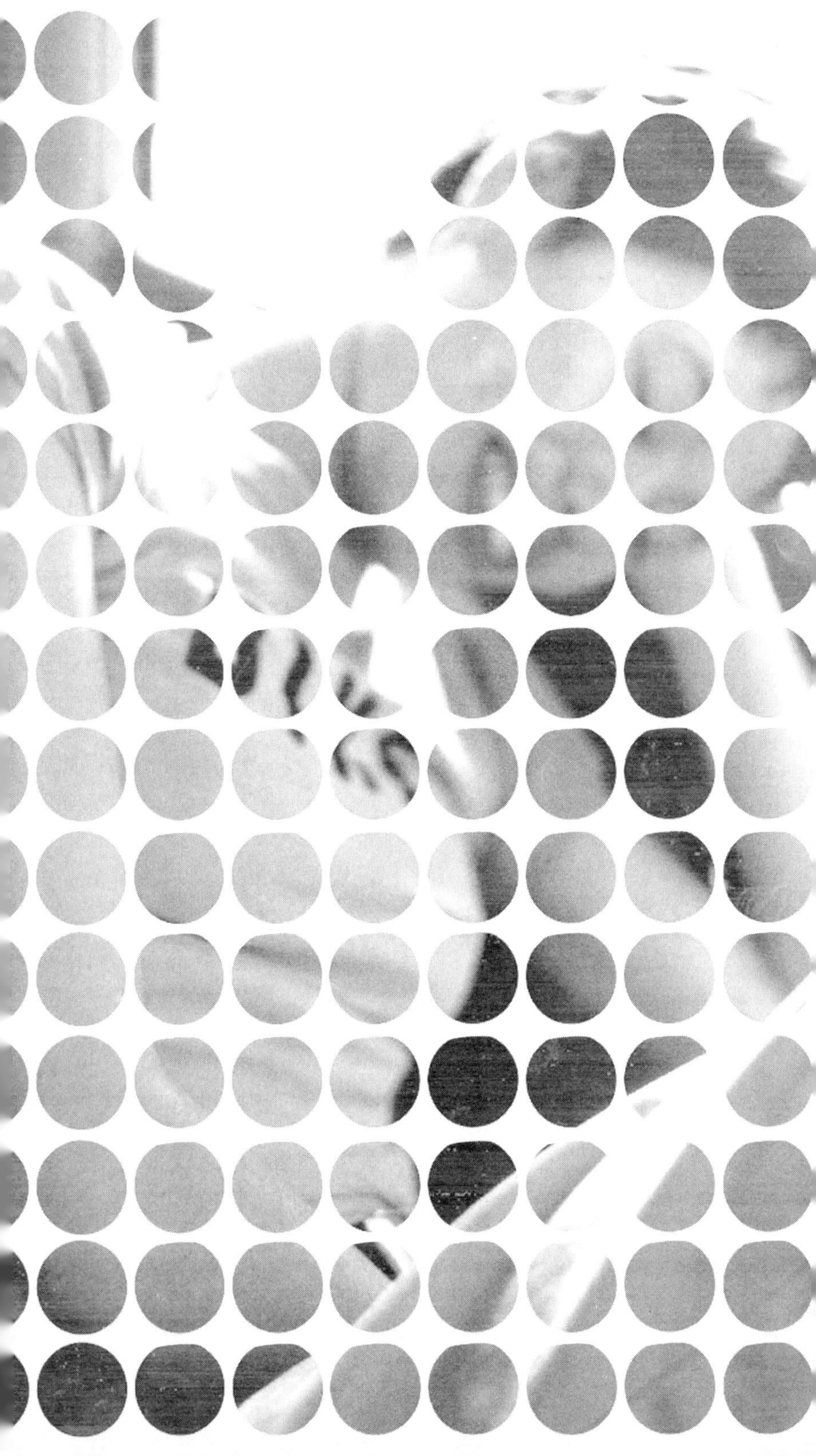

Jason Roe, 20
Gaithersburg, MD

I grew up deeply involved in various Washington, D.C., youth cultures. This piece was included in my 'zine *Kill the Robot #6*, part of a split 'zine with *Girlfiend* (by Christa in Hampshire, Mass., and *Simba* (by Vique in Brighton, England). *Kill the Robot* went up to eight issues, with thousands of copies circulating internationally. This 'zine was just one project in a long string of mad-scientist concoctions and realized pipe dreams. After its demise I worked on *Strange Fruit*, created with Ted Young-Ing, which showcased underground art and culture. I now live in New York City and am trying to kick it over, eat well, and have fun.

This is to me

This is about me

This is for me on those days that I feel dumb and afraid. When I think that I am wrong or immoral or bad or whatever else might be lurking in my mind. This is to say to hell with all of that to the idea that I can't be who I am. This is about the times I felt afraid or embarrassed or the times I felt proud when I didn't talk about being a queer too much. This is for me when I feel abnormal. Because right now I feel wonderful. Right now I feel natural. Right now I know that they are all wrong. Right now I know that I am not here to produce children. Right now I know that my only worth is not in the breeding of humans. Now I know that ideas of me being non natural are stupid and ill conceived. The idea that love goes only one way. The idea that I can't show emotion to a person of my gender. All too silly. All too wrong. Now i know that who I am is not based on what I do with my genitals or with my hands or what I do with my words. It is based on important things. This is for those days when I care whether my arms are around a man or a woman. This is for the days when I think it matters. This is for the days when I think that I can't live a 'normal' life. This is for the days when I am criticized. This is for the days when I am attacked. This is for the times when I am afraid to walk down the street. This is for the times I got hurt and humiliated. This is for being called fag. This is for my love. This is for the gay agenda. This is the for the idea that I am only a sexual being. This is for the idea that I only want to have sex and I never want to take walks or sit and read while you are in the room. This is for the idea that I only relate with my genitals. This is for the idea that queerness only has to do with sex. This is for you telling me it is insignificant. This is for me because I am real. This is for me most of all because I have the right to be happy. **And this is also just as much for you**

Ahimsa Timoteo Bodhrán, 23
South Bronx, N.Y. and Oakland, Califas, Aztlán, Turtle Island

I was born in 1974 on *El Día de la Madre* in the South Bronx to an Irish Catholic mother and a mixed-blood Sefardí (Spanish-Arab-African-Jewish) father. Currently I live in Oakland, Califas, Aztlán, Turtle Island, where in addition to being the editor of both a men-of-color-loving-men-of-color anthology and an anthology about men of color who have survived different forms of violence, I am also the author of a forthcoming solo book, *Yerbabuena/Mala yerba, All My Roots Need Rain: Mixed Blood Poetry & Prose.* A member of RAWI (Radius of Arab-American Writers, Inc.) and NASAWI (The New Association of Sephardi/Mizrahi Artists and Writers International), I have spoken, performed, and led workshops across what is now known by some as the United States, and my written work has appeared in numerous publications. I am a survivor, *curandero*-in-training, and (grand)father/mother-to-be.

was ich bin

for Aurora Levins Morales & Lani Ka`ahumanu

i am the jew   el converso   un judío árabe y africano   ein jude the sefardí/ashkenazi who does not go ta synagogue   not even on high holidays   who lights shabbat candles in silence every friday night   not knowing why   bcuz he wuz hidden   he is a secret a geheimnis only now unfolding   who hears the shofar   distant against a backdrop of stars   points of light which guide his people   their lives lived in exile   along their eternal journey   home

i am the catholic   the christian red-headed green-eyed altarboy   irish priest-in-training   the curandero who does not go ta confession   bcuz he has nothing ta confess   save his life which is apparently worth little   here   or in the hereafter   but who builds altars ta his ancestors in his room   their pictures on the wall   candles lit   incense burning   offerings at their feet next ta a crucifix he himself built   who crosses himself each time an ambulance goes by   a firetruck   a church   each time he hears the passing   of a friend

i am the person of color   mestizo   blanco   café con leche who does not remember racism except his own   bcuz he wuz told he wuz white n believed it   whose family pulled him out of the sun for fear he would turn braun   como chocolate   como su papá   como su abuelos   calling him el puertorriqueño   making him ashamed of his round body   olive und braun   who tried ta wash his color away   his mamá always wondering why he took so long   en el baño   the water always running down   the drain   but who now longs ta b dark   darker   who waits for the sun ta kiss him   braun him   yes burn him   but who does not hate the winters that pale him as he once did

i am the queer the bisexual el joto una mariposa who does not want ta march in pride parades or go ta bars or meetings or sign petitions but instead spread his wings n fly bcuz he has no name for his love save hers or his or theirs nor does he want any who does not date white people n them infuriated by this it being an auction n them already having placed their bid who just wants ta take care of his gente his brothers n sisters of color whom he loves in whose history he walks in whose voices he sings

i am the working-class person poor person struggling person who does not talk about class bcuz the books on marx n capitalism r not written for him n he can not afford degrees enuf ta prove he is an expert on his own oppression but who remembers the government food he ate the bougie white children he tried ta emulate who writes knowing his mother can n can not read who writes knowing besides himself y su hermano y su abuela y una madrina no one in his family reads whose history whose traditions r oral spoken n remembered

i am the disabled the dyslexic sin ruedas who does not use wheelchair ramps bcuz he can walk "fine" but with words he has trouble it is books n forms assignments n conversations that r his barriers whose disability is invisible except ta others similarly blessed whose gift it is ta always come up with new words new ways of speaking being the likes of which the world has never seen nor heard

i am the person who does not fit in who is alone who is

many who is legion who blends in who sticks out who speaks out bcuz I am often denied community i have no home save this body n even that is under attack

grown-up

for Sapphire, who wrote me a permission slip

as a little boy growing up, i used ta sit in the bathtub, take the little spikey thing u put soap on, n lay on it, press my little pre-pubescent dick on it hard, impale myself, sometimes until i bled. then i'd take it, bloodied n bruised, n tuck it between my legs, standing in front of the mirror, pushing the fat that wuz my chest together, seeing what it would b like ta have cleavage, thinking perhaps i could escape my fate by becoming a woman, i wondered what it'd b like ta have a pussy, what it would b like ta cut it off, ta simply not have it around no more.

as a little boy growing up, i starved myself. i remember doing over fours hours of exercise each day, eating only watermelon n starkist tuna from a can for weeks on end, trying ta puke but not being able ta stomach the convulsions, being depressed/ashamed whenever we had ta go shopping for school clothes, clothes that would not fit. i hated the month of august for this very reason.

as a little boy growing up, i spent my summers in the sun, laying out all day, trying to b darker, wanting ta b whiter. i spent hours in the bathroom, trying ta wash away my body, my skin color, my sex, contemplating suicide, homicide, genocide, that which i could bring about, that which others were capable of.

as a little boy growing up, i

used ta stick myself with pencils, jab myself with pens, trying ta stop the thoughts, trying ta make my bad n evil, dark n dirty, fat n faggy, boy body, go away.

it didn't. but a piece of me, a piece of that glorious childhood i wuz supposed ta have, it did. it did go away. n some things, like toys left at the beach when u'r on vacation, r lost forever. forever is a very long time. a very long time, indeed.

Alegría Sonata Barclay, 23

I am a 23-year-old mixed-race queer poet of Vietnamese/Scottish/Swedish descent. I grew up in the Middle East, Africa, Europe, and North America and now live in California. I'm still trying to figure out what home means and is, and where I will ultimately reside. Hopefully, somewhere inside of myself. I believe that writing, art, and expression are the most powerful vehicles for social change and justice. Poetry can be and is revolutionary. Within the confines of the page I try to express the voices of people who are silenced, marginalized, oppressed, or no longer living. I consider myself primarily a love poet, because I believe that all revolution and resistance should come from a place of love, even though they may start from a place of anger. In my work I explore the intersections between love, anger, desire, sorrow, and faith.

what are you?
the not-so-definitive answer
(inspired by jennifer lisa vest and thich nhat hanh)

i.
human
a virgo
a woman
a lover
a lesbian
a bitch
a poet
a person
a perfectionist
a traveler
a teacher
an artist
an activist
a fill-in-the-blank
add-a-box
other
the other
the other
the other

ii.
but why do you ask
you already call me
ugly or exotic
funny-looking
and freak
you call me

geisha girl with a hint of barbie
beautiful but with too much yellow
too little white
not enough slant
too little breasts
beautiful but
not enough
not enough
to make it matter
you call me
traitor and
child of a tramp
so you married a white man
so you mixed the blood
so you broke tradition
polluted the lineage
polluted polluted polluted the line
you call me pollution
dirty   the downfall
of eastern civilization
of western civilization
the end of purity
the beginning of moral breakdown
the unacceptable
the unbelievable
the white man's burden
the white daddy's disease
the repercussion of rape
the fruit of the forbidden
you name me
other other other

iii.
what i am is
all of the above
in this body
i am all of the above
and i am what my momma calls me
“the only good thing to come out of that war”
the only beautiful thing to be born
i am the living legacy of war
i am sorrow
i am death
i am the screaming faces streaked with blood
i am the misplaced eighteen-year-old from iowa
i am the president one step removed
i am nameless and buried beneath land
i cannot call my home
i am my uncle exploding
as i step on a mine
i am a woman crying as i watch his remains
fall to earth
i am a monk burning bright
i am the people’s revolution
i am hope
i am ho chi minh
heavy with doubt
i am the final heartbeat
the fall of saigon
the last helicopter to leave
i am a boat person
clinging to mist
i am the last one alive in my family
at the refugee camp

i am an immigrant
i am exile
this is what i am
the offspring of ideology
a product of war
but
i am also
the product of love
of one vietnamese woman
one white man
a testimony to touch
i am creation
i am life

iv.
what am i?
i am what comes after
i am becoming
i am finding my way
in spite of human havoc
i am seeking
i am the buddha to be
the blessed one
the breath between every breath
the bell that chimes within
the heart's home
i am compassion
and prayer without pausing
peace within every step
i am the end of the other
i am the meaning of my name

Anonymous, 22
USA

I could be anyone, anywhere. I could be your sister, your brother, your cousin, mother, father, friend. I could be the kid you called "faggot" in grade school, the girl you pinned against the chain-link fence, hissing "dyke" before leaving her afraid to walk home alone ever again. I could be someone you know, or someone you don't; someone you never wanted to be. But the things I faced as a low-income, queer, punk kid are things we all face at one time or another. We have got to help each other heal. We have got to stand up for one another. We have got to see what makes us similar and honor the things that make us different. These poems are for the ones who landed back on the streets, the ones who went to jail, the ones who stayed hooked, who hit the bottle again, the ones who went out for cigarettes and never came back. They are for everyone who searches for self in a world that hides it from us.

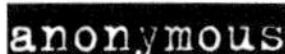

where the dead live

she could have had so many lives
—dorianne laux

i didn't know where we were going
laid on the backseat in my ratted blue sweatshirt
and hated everything
the stuccoed strip malls
slouching palm trees
and the impossibly persistent sunshine
that made things look even more dirty and desperate

at the asylum i faced off with a nurse
in a room with no windows
she wanted me to strip
and i wanted to blow up
the entire goddamn world
but piece by piece
she took me apart
til i was naked and shaking
on the carpet
then she cinched an i.d. bracelet
around my bloody wrist
and pulled me down a maze of locking doors—
each one clicked behind us—
finally we reached the neon lit heart of the hospital
everything bleached anemic whites and greens

nurses talked out loud like i couldn't hear
she didn't
                    no, she really did, look

and rotated my arm to see
then they laid me on a cot in a dark room
and i knew
this was the realm of the dead
the last door
had snapped
shut

problem kids: an elegy for kurt cobain

we sat in the back of class
with our army boots
blue hair
and faded black t-shirts
like flashing neon signs
that said
stay the fuck   away
we penned messages on our backpacks:
anarchy rocks
satan rules
i hate you
yes   you
asshole

we plugged our ears with headphones
and cranked up guns n roses
AC/DC *megadeth metallica nirvana*
so everyone could hear their crashing symphonies
of guitar chords piled on drumbeats
and wild screaming rage
we wore dark eyeliner

smoked stolen cigarettes
came to school drunk and stoned and
didn't try to hide it—
we were fifteen
and daydreamed armageddon
we wanted to watch the whole world
grind to a halt, we wanted it
to be bloody

but when our rock star idol
shot himself
one bullet straight through the back of his mouth
it was like the image of our own suicides
plastered across all the tabloids
and we were strangely
sad
it occured to us
that loss required
something to lose
that we wanted to find out
what it was we had

Liz Gaden, 16
Round Rock, TX

I live near Austin, Texas, and am a 16-year-old high school junior. I plan to major in music performance in college. I play the piano, guitar, and I sing. I have two older brothers and tons of cats and dogs. "Be who you are and will be, learn to cherish that boisterous black angel that drives you up one day and down another." —Audre Lorde

I was only 13 when...

I was only 13 when I realized I was gay. Over the previous few months I had slowly, not even noticing it, become intrigued by gay people. They just seemed interesting to me. It didn't even seem significant that I always thought that I wanted to have a fling with a woman before I got married. Finally, it started to dawn on me: I might be gay. For two months I constantly thought, *What if I'm gay...I can't be gay...I'm not gay...but gosh, she sure is cute!*

Then one day I looked in the mirror and told myself, *Liz, you're not gay. Well, Liz...you're 95% sure you're not gay, OK, just 90%, but that's pretty darn sure!* The next day I was watching TV and suddenly realized that the person I wanted sitting beside me would *not* be a man but a woman. From that moment I have accepted my sexuality.

I never fathomed how difficult it would be to keep that part of my life a secret, especially in junior high. Every day I'd hear gay jokes and slanders coming from everyone I knew. It tore me up inside. I never had been very popular, and I was always made fun of because I was smart, wore glasses, and was quiet. I was a nerd; I still am, I guess. Although none of the name-calling was directed toward me, I still felt each word was made just for me.

The summer before high school was an emotional hell. I had nothing to keep my mind occupied with, so I contemplated suicide constantly. My parents came near to discovering my secret. I'm surprised they didn't, considering I listened to Melissa Etheridge religiously. They read one of my E-mails that said in a roundabout way that I was gay. My parents confronted me, and I freaked out. I locked myself in my room for the rest of the day, and I'm sure I would have killed myself right then if I'd had anything to do it with in my room. I sat and cried all day because I was scared—scared of what might happen if they knew. I had no idea how they would react. I wasn't ready to tell them.

When I entered high school, things got worse. On top of being gay, I was a freshman. I had been finding my solace on the Internet reading other writings by gay youth and guidelines about coming out to your family. One day I was sitting in geometry crying, and I realized I needed to talk to someone. So I went to see one of the school counselors. She was a godsend. I began writing in a journal, and she would read it every time I saw her. Eventually I built up the courage to come out to her in my journal. (It was National Coming Out Day; it felt appropriate.) She took it well, and I felt I finally had an outlet for my feelings, no matter how small that outlet may have been.

Then the inevitable happened. My parents read my journal. I was outed. I was terrified. My mother came into the kitchen one night and asked me to follow her. I walked into the room where we keep our computer, and she had two chairs set up. I knew what was to follow immediately. My stomach dropped to the floor; I will never forget that feeling. When she told me that she had read my journal, I began to cry and so did she.

Over the next few weeks I talked my parents into driving me to Austin to attend a meeting of the local gay youth group, Out Youth Austin. The first day I went I was terrified. I knew I wouldn't know anyone, and I'd never even met another gay person in my life. I had no idea what to expect. As it turned out, I met the nicest people, and I started going there every week. I didn't really get to be friends with anyone until the next summer. I've never been too social. After that, though, everything seemed to fall into place.

A few months into my sophomore year two people from my school came to a meeting the same night as me, and eventually we all became good friends. Over the rest of the year they gave me the self-confidence to be out, and I began wearing my freedom rings and other rainbow accessories to school. The only problem I encountered was a threat from a student toward the beginning of the year, but that was taken care of by the school's administration. And one of my big, tough lesbian friends threatened him back, which made me proud. By the end of the year I was known as a lesbian, and I started dating, although I wasn't very good at getting dates. I have gotten much better at that, though. My parents have become so accepting that when my mother and I are out in town she points out pretty girls to me. She even baked a cake for Ellen DeGeneres's coming out!

Being gay and in high school is still hard sometimes, but I have so many accepting friends that I don't even notice I'm different most of the time. I can't wait to go to college and meet new people. I am a little scared about leaving my family and living somewhere far away, but I know it will be worth it because of the friends that I'll make. I have one piece of advice for other gay teens out there: High school is never easy, but it doesn't last forever. Never give up. Four years ago I wanted to die because of my sexuality. Now I can't wait to go on living. Realizing I was gay was the best thing that ever happened to me.

Chris Cotrina, 19
Houston, TX

My name is Chris Cotrina. I'm 19, Hispanic, and gay. For the first time in my life I feel no shame in telling the world I'm Hispanic and gay. It was hard for me to tell my parents the truth about myself. I always felt I was putting my family down if I didn't try not to be gay. Throughout my life I have met many different people who have helped me to accept and love myself for who I am. Eventually I'd like to start an outreach program to educate Hispanic parents to better understand their gay kids. There are many outreach programs for English-speaking people, but in Texas the majority of Hispanics don't speak English. I also want to find love and get married. And I want to have children.

Don’t Ask Because I Won’t Tell

When I’m ready,
I’ll tell.
But for now,
please don’t ask.

Andromeda, 18
West Springfield, Mass.

I am an 18-year-old gay male from West Springfield, Mass., attending a two-year college in Manassas, Va. I am a liberal arts major and have serious interests in both music production and photography. I am fascinated with disco culture and love disco music as well as many other musical styles. The two people I admire most are Peter Tchaikovsky (famous Russian romantic composer of the late 1800s) and Andy Warhol (famous pop-culture artist). Coincidentally, both were also gay. Quote: "Where words leave off, music begins...."

Grateful

A 16-year-old gay boy stands in front of his bathroom mirror. His newly divorced parents have torn his already shaken heart to pieces. His father's worsening alcoholism weighs heavily on his mind, and his mother's new boyfriend poses a physical threat to him. Failing grades and homophobia make school unbearable. The boy just stands there. Silent.

He wants so much to talk to his mother in hopes that she will listen and allow him to release the burdens from his shoulders. He hesitates, though. He already knows her lecturing response. "There will always be people worse off than you. So be grateful," his mother all too often repeats. And he knows it's true.

He slams his fists against the mirror in frustration. He is disgusted by his dreary reflection. Large darkening bags stain the skin beneath his eyes. He realizes how ravaged his body has become. He begins to sob, silently, uncontrollably. "Son, there will always be people worse off than you," he hears his father saying. And he knows it's true.

But the pain is still there. He grabs a small white bottle and runs to his bedroom.

* * *

Scanning the morning newspaper, the father of a 16-year-old girl comes across a tragic article about a young boy found dead in his room by his mother just two days before. As his daughter comes down the stairs to head off to school he takes her aside and points out the article. "Honey, I want you to always remember one thing," he says. "Remember that there will always be someone, somewhere who has it worse than you. So be grateful."

She swallows her own pain and nods, because she knows it's true.

Mollie Biewald, 15
Shutesbury, Mass.

I am a 15-year-old dyke artist and activist. I've got flaming pink hair and a passion for genderfuck in both directions. I escaped school a month into ninth grade, after two years of daily queer bashing because I didn't look enough "like a girl" for my rural town of 1000. I moved to Boston and am now taking classes all over—Harvard, art schools, and local community colleges. I love working on my zine, making movies (super-8 and video), and doing other artsy things. I plan to run off to San Francisco as soon as possible to find a career and continue doing art.

Bent, ink on cardboard, 6” x 6”, 1998

Butch, mixed media, 7” x 5” x 3”, 1999

Anonymous, 17
Northeast, USA

I am a 17-year-old female-to-male transgendered queer. I am also a nerdy bisexual activist and aspiring writer. I wrote "Letter From a Butch" when I was finally beginning to confront gender identity issues that I had actively avoided dealing with for a long time. I woke up one day and decided to stop all the pretending and be true to myself. This piece reflects that time in my life. I am now in the process of starting to live my life as a man, which feels more right to me. I look forward to the day when my real name can accompany my writing without worry!

Letter From a Butch

Everything and everyone has told me loudly, in ways both subtle and direct, that it's not OK for me to be like this...it's not OK to walk firmly with a determined stride...it's not OK to feel more comfortable in boots and overalls or a jacket and tie than in a skirt and heels...it's not OK to love women, and if you must be a lesbian, it's sure as hell not OK to be a "dykey" lesbian...it's not OK to want to touch more than to be touched, to want to hold a woman protectively, to be more aggressive and less soft...it's not OK to want to pass as a man sometimes, to wear your hair short, to talk confidently, to refuse to drop your eyes...it's not OK to fit stereotypes (e.g., that of the mannish lesbian), to enjoy un-p.c. roles feminism has deemed antifeminist. In short, it's not OK to be BUTCH. Butch is a scary word. It's what you don't want to be called, what you are afraid to admit you are. It's what makes you stand out in a crowd when you'd rather not be noticed, what challenges people's comfort and their ideas about gender, what some queers wish would disappear so that normal gay and lesbian folks can assimilate into straight society and become invisible.

Everywhere I look I see messages telling me it's not OK to be who I am. I am so tired of trying to be feminine, and I'm angry that I've been conditioned to believe I should fit into a role that doesn't come naturally to me. I've been socialized as a girl. These assumptions have become a part of me. It's a daily struggle to not make my voice all high-pitched and sweet when I talk to men, to not put earrings on just because the figure in the mirror looks too much like a boy. These are automatic—but not biological—reactions. They are the result of the brainwashing we go through from the day we are born. Sometimes I wonder if the government secretly slips these gender codes into milk cartons to ensure that every child grows up with a rigid idea of what gender is, and with tremendous guilt if they don't fit into their assigned role.

* * *

And then there's you. You came into my life, the first person who has ever celebrated my butchness, who has not been outwardly or secretly uncomfortable with my behavior or appearance. You are not ashamed of me, you don't shake your head like you don't understand how I could be this way. The only person to want me as a friend and a lover *for* my butchness, not *in spite of* it.

I have hidden, denied, ignored, and camouflaged so much of who I am. I thought it was enough to learn to be comfortable with my lesbianism, but it's not. I need to be comfortable not just with loving women, but with *how* I love them and how I show that love. I need to feel confident and even proud in my butch existence, not just when I'm holding you but also when I'm walking alone on the streets, when we're at the movies, when I go to a family reunion, when I'm sitting in the classroom.

You asked me if I wanted you to make love to me as I did to you and I told you "No." I need to explain why. I am not yet fully secure in my butchness, as it relates to myself, the world, and you. Your tongue or fingers can melt me, can make me moan, can turn soft every hard place in my body, heart, and soul. You can make me feel like a silly little girl. But it is not until I feel strong, confident, sturdy, solid, and in control that I can feel comfortable letting you see me weak, unsure, wavering, soft, and out-of-control. I have to feel and accept my butchness fully before I can let it be challenged, conquered, or peeled away, even for a little while.

There is so much right now that is new to me. Above all, I am new to feeling accepted for being the awkward, dorky, thick-legged, soft butch that I am, and I am new to walking down the street with someone who is not ashamed of me or who makes me feel ashamed of myself. I am new to feeling that, as much as the expressions on the faces of the heads that I turn every day are those of hatred or disgust, I can count on there being one person whose expression will always be loving, whose eyes are seductive and respectful, not violent or repulsed.

I'm not a victim or martyr, and I've hardly suffered compared to most in this world. I feel fortunate that my heart is not heavy with pain. But like many of my sisters, I am growing a hard, hard stone wall around myself. This wall, I need it terribly. And things are not getting easier as I grow older. You've warned me yourself that as I grow into myself as a butch dyke, I can expect more, not fewer, confrontations with fear and hatred and ignorance (and aren't all three the same?). I need this wall to fend off spears, to drown out the sound of the angry words thrown at me. I pick them up and build the wall out of them.

I need you to help me make it strong. But I also need to reassure my heart that it's OK to let you in. The same holes that would be big enough for you to crawl through are big enough to allow in hurt that my heart's not sure she's ready for. I don't know how to let you in without letting in pain. I'm consulting my architect. Maybe we can figure this one out, because I'm dying for some company in here. Please, let's never forget that we're in this together; that as much shit as we have to deal with, we can deal with it together. Let us never allow the fear, the pain, the struggle to overshadow our love for one another.

I miss you. Only two more weeks until I hold you in my arms again.

With love,
Your adoring butch

S. Asher Hanley, 21

I have had many names, but the one I have settled on is Samtanis Asher Hanley. I am a 21-year-old queer boi of mixed heritage (human-melting-pot–style) and intersexed physicality. An avid photographer, painter, musician, and writer, I have spent the past three years trying to pin myself down in art. I'm still working on that—I think the journey and the destination are one and the same. I'm beginning to believe life is the process of learning about oneself and trying to understand and learn about others. My highest aspirations are to be unabashedly myself for the rest of my life and to do my part, in whatever way I can, to make the world a gentler place for everyone, especially those of us who live outside the bounds of its narrow definition of "normal." I also want to adopt all kinds of stray dogs and cats. My more worldly aspirations include getting married, learning Vietnamese and Chinese, and finishing my computer science degree within the next three years.

s. asher hanley

Different: My Experiences as an Intersexed Gay Boy

OK, think about this one: You're driving around the city on a Friday night, about 8:30 P.M., and you see this skinny boy dressed in black with a backpack and neatly gelled hair. Maybe he doesn't have the most masculine walk you ever saw, maybe he even swishes a little, and you notice when he glances at a man on a motorcycle. You're with four of your friends and they're cracking jokes about him.... So what do you do?

Last night I was that skinny boy in black. The car passed me on a road in Syracuse. A girl shouted from the front passenger-side window, "Faggot!" I admit, it rattled me a little, even though chances are she wouldn't have said word one to me if she didn't have a thousand pounds of steel insulation around her. Maybe driving in a car makes people forget what it's like to be human. Regardless, this assault simply reminded me, yet again, that I'm different.

I guess it happens to straight boys too sometimes—those who aren't quite up to the "standard" of masculinity that our culture dictates. They get harassed in gym lockers and in front of frat houses like the rest of us. They're certainly not immune. But it happens most often, though, to people like myself—those whose bodies and hearts lie beyond the limited scope of understanding exhibited by people like the girl who yelled at me from a moving car.

It didn't make me angry, really, to be called that. It saddened and bemused me, though, that our culture encourages that kind of behavior. It hurts my soul to see people act so mindlessly, so automatically. They manifest the programming of our culture so blatantly. Our country is negative about a lot of things. I hear people make both subtle and overt racist comments on a daily basis; same goes with sexist comments, homophobic comments, and comments that deride diverse spiritual beliefs.

We are expected to fit into neatly packaged and narrowly defined categories. Even our mannerisms are marketed to us. We're constantly being reminded of how we "should" behave: Men should like sports; women should like shopping. Men should pay attention to things such as fishing and beer; women should obsess about their weight, hair, and nails. "And never the twain shall meet," as it's said.

This is all part of the reason people like me are subjected to life-altering surgery before they're even old enough to talk. I, like one out of every 500 infants, was born intersexed. This means I'm neither here nor there, biologically speaking—I don't fit neatly into one of the expected options ("male" or "female"). Every day, on campus and off, I pass for the average queer (if there is such a thing). Among gay boys, I am capable of passing until someone finds out what I am underneath my clothes, and then, once again, I become the outsider. This has defined my existence for so long that it is easy for me to forget I can be accepted at all.

Right now my greatest struggle is to accept myself as a desirable, even a marriageable human being. By that I mean, people in our culture grow up expecting to marry a man or a woman, even if they're gay. They don't expect to marry someone who is intersexed, let alone someone who defies the system of sex and gender on which our society is based. Not only am I physically androgynous, but also I staunchly believe that our expected gender roles are mere constructions.

I don't believe that men should be any more restricted from making lives as homemakers than women should be restricted from making lives as construction workers. Women's work and men's work should be one in the same: people's work. Every human being should have access to a full range of choices. There is no biological justification for any restriction in this way—be it by gender, race, creed, and so on.

Still, I wonder sometimes where I'll find my place in this culture. I know what I want—to be an independent computer network engineer and homemaker, where my role as a homemaker will take precedence. But sometimes it's hard to imagine finding a place where I can fit that way. I don't understand why some people think it's disgraceful that I should want this. It isn't. They point to my being intersexed, being gay, and being a rather "feminine boy." All I can say to them is that I would still want this life if I were a standard "masculine" heterosexual man. None of these things have any more to do with sex or gender than fish have to do with bicycles.

Which brings to me to the other struggle I have faced most often: How open should I be in a such a dichotomous world? I am generally open with anyone who asks me whether I'm male or female (and you'd be surprised how many people will ask). I am glad that people ask and usually answer them honestly, as long as it seems safe to discuss. If it doesn't seem safe, I just say, "I'm a boy. I just reached puberty late." My friends all know, of course. I tell them because being intersexed is more than just a biological reality; it's part of who I am. I am open with my friends. In turn, they've been absolutely invaluable in my journey toward self-acceptance.

As for acquaintances, they are harder to deal with. I wasn't sure whether to tell my classmates last semester, and if I did, how I should bring it up. At first I thought I wouldn't, but I realized that every conversation I have with people is an opportunity to educate. People will never understand those things to which they haven't been exposed. I learned to be brave. I figured the quickest path to change is understanding and the quickest path to understanding is visibility. So I became visible. I wrote a paper arguing against neonatal cosmetic surgeries on intersexed children, and it was received well. Still, most people have only the faintest idea, if any, of what the word "intersexed" means. They know neither the realities of our bodies nor the morally reprehensible treatment we receive at the hands of the medical profession.

For what it's worth, I am mystified by the rigidity not only of sex and gender but also of gender roles in our culture. These roles are arbitrary constructs of patriarchal culture, yet they're simply accepted as truths by the masses. They permeate our lives—so entrenched, they've become invisible. We are blinded by them as if we were staring into the sun. Most people seem to live their lives without ever questioning them.

In a way I have been blessed with an intersexed life. Not to say my biology makes me any more free of these gendered expectations—it doesn't. In fact, doctors would like to see me adhere even more rigidly to my expected role than other people do. But my upbringing has afforded me the ability to see the pros and cons of various options and to consider my own identity more deeply than most people ever realize they can. My biology only makes it clear that, at a more basic level, it makes as little sense to define only two sexes as it does to define only two genders. I believe I am, for better or for worse, living proof that human beings are far more complicated than that.

reate.

Nzinga Akili, 24
New York, N.Y.

Nzinga Akili is a psuedonym meaning, "She is beauty, she is courage, she is wisdom." I am a law student and an African-American, Bi-Sexual, Womon-Loving Womon of Art, Music, and all things Spiritual and Peaceful.

To Know

She prefers to steal a glimpse before savoring
the silken perfume...she ignores my teasing
and dares me to withstand her lingual caress
my fingers tangled within her locks
I begin burning and I extend
as she sinks into
forbidden fruit....

suddenly I am water rising
whipping washing purifying
and old moans become
new bonfires ripping
through my
lungs

Gina de Vries, 15
San Francisco, Calif.

I am a poet and queer youth activist about to enter tenth grade at The Urban School. I am the "Hey! Baby!" columnist for *Curve* magazine, and I self-publish a 'zine called *Luscious Thoughts/Talk Normal*. I am also a member of several queer and youth-oriented activist groups, including the Lesbian Gay Bisexual Transgender Advisory Committee to the San Francisco Human Rights Commission. When I am not running around madly or writing, I fancy hanging out with my buddies and window-shopping at thrift stores.

gina de vries

Coming Out in Middle School

I first began to come out when I was 11. In terms of my family, I was fortunate because my parents have always been accepting of my sexual identity. It was really great to have their backing, especially considering that a lot of lesbian, gay, bisexual, and transgender people don't have that kind of family support. I come from a political, staunchly liberal family; I guess you could say I inherited my parents' socialist genes. However, the school I was going to when I came out was immensely different from my home situation.

I was in sixth grade and attending a Catholic school in San Francisco when I came out to a small group of people. (I was actually raised in an agnostic household, but the Catholic school was three blocks away from where I lived.) My fellow students had already assumed I was a queer because I defended queer people and got angry at folks in my class when they said the word "faggot." So of course they were making accusations about my sexuality left and right. Still, I didn't feel comfortable coming out to all of them.

During this time I started attending LYRIC, the Lavender Youth Recreation and Information Center, a wonderful program and hang-out space for LGBT youth in San Francisco. Just hanging out with other queer youth and finding a place where I could get support was incredible. Programs that give queer youth a space to be safe are really important, and I know that finding LYRIC helped me out a lot.

The next year I was in seventh grade. At that point I was tired of being harassed, and I had gotten to a place in my life where I could actually deal with the harassment and stand up to people who hurt me. I realized I could only be happy if I was honest with the people around me. So at the age of 12 I came out to my entire elementary school, which included grades K-8.

The reaction I encountered was not good. I got a lot of really rude questions and comments from kids. It got to the point where the little kids would run away from me whenever I passed them in the school yard because they'd been told I was a dangerous person. That hurt so much. Now, admittedly, not *everyone* was overtly homophobic—some people just had questions because they had never met anyone who they knew was queer before. It felt really good to be teaching people, but overall, middle school was not a good experience.

Right now I'm going into the tenth grade at The Urban School of San Francisco. I'm completely out there and have never once been harassed. I'm really amazed. If anything, the kids I'm around are proud of me for the work I'm doing in the queer community. I feel safe and happy at Urban, and I wish every school could be like that. Sadly, that isn't the case.

Even though I had to deal with a lot of harassment in middle school, it was all worth it. I learned how to deal with harassment and how to educate people. Now I'm in a safe place, and I'm able to be honest about who I am. That is what is most important to me.

reate.

Ryan P. Reyes, 22
Manila, Philippines

I was born and raised in Manila, Philippines. I immigrated to the United States in 1997. I received my B.A. in history from the University of the Philippines in 1998. I was a member of UP Babaylan, a gay school organization. I am currently taking courses at New York University. Part-time, I flip burgers in a fast-food restaurant and run the register in a supermarket. In both jobs I can practice my English. On the Internet I am a community leader for Geocities WestHollywood where I have a personal Web site, http://www.geocities.com/WestHollywood/2251/.

Proud to Be an FOB

It's morning in New York City, and it's exactly the opposite time where I grew up, in the Phillipines. I am a gay Asian immigrant, and it is quite difficult adjusting to a foreign country. Being a minority within a minority, I find that there are no role models for me. I look up pages of *XY, OUT, Genre*, and *The Advocate*, and all I see are articles suited for the "gay white male." I further browse the magazine sections in the hopes of finding a magazine or even an article in a magazine suited for me. I see something that has an Asian cover. I quickly grab it and look in the pages thoroughly. Oops, it had some nude pictures of Asians. Funny, though, that the front cover said, "Presenting a Positive Image of Asian Men."

I immigrated to the United States with my family in 1997. That was three years ago. During those years I learned a lot. It seems that being gay and Asian in America, one has to uphold his self-respect on two fronts. The first is being Asian. Contrary to what many believe, Asians are also discriminated against. I can still remember the number of times I was called "Ching" in school for having slanted eyes. One terrifying event also was when I was walking down 14th Street and an old man started harassing me. He just started shouting that I should go back to my country. When I tell this to my friends they quickly dismiss it as "Ugggh, only in New York."

The second front is being gay. Even in the Philippines, where I grew up, I suffered many teasings about my homosexuality. I studied in an exclusive Catholic school for boys. Day after day my classmates would gang up on me, teasing me for my "girl-ish manners." But I found solace through my friends. They were also gay, and they also suffered the constant teasings that I underwent. But the turning point in my youth was coming out of the closet when I was 13. Hard to believe, but I told my parents.

It took them a while, but eventually they accepted me. But here in America everything is different. It is true that the teasing stopped. But it also seems that I am not included in the gay community. Apathy is just as bad as hate. I know that there are some gay Asian organizations here, but most of these organizations are for the "East-West friendship." I find nothing wrong with this, but where are the political gay Asians who lobby for gay Asian empowerment? Where are the gay Asian youths who meet at least once a week to share stories, bond, and simply get together?

I am what people would call an "FOB"—fresh off the boat. And not knowing anyone in a foreign country is extremely terrifying. You're quickly introduced to a new culture that you know nothing about. Here they have terms like *rice queen, potato queen, sticky rice*, and *banana*. Gay American culture insists that I am rice and my boyfriend should be a potato. My skin should be smooth, brown, and hairless, and his should resemble that of Wonder bread. If I go against this, I am labeled *sticky rice* and condemned as going against the natural way. I am introduced to films such as *M. Butterfly* and *The Wedding Banquet,* in which Asians are devoted to their respective white American partner. I am further introduced to literature such as Norman Wong's *Cultural Revolution* and Ricardo Ramos's *Flipping,* in which gay Asians strictly desire white men. There are also the independent films like Tony Ayres's *China Dolls* and Raymond Yeung's *Yellow Fever* where, again, Asians limit themselves to white men. Where are my role models? Where are the images of brotherhood—and sisterhood—within our community?

I have been in America for three years already. Yet I still am perceived as the naive Asian boy that people refer to as an FOB. But I ask you, *Where and who are the Asian Americans that I should exemplify?* I guess I should only look to myself as my role model.

If what I have seen here in America is the norm for Asian Americans, let me be the first to tell you, “No thank you. I’m proud to be an FOB!”

Jerome C. Boyce, 17
Brooklyn, N.Y.

Hi, my name is Jerome Carlton Boyce. I am 17 years old and the cousin of best-selling author James Earl Hardy, who wrote *B-Boy Blues* (Alyson, 1994). I am trying to write a book now, but it is not easy. It is called *Shades: Color it in*, and it will be followed by a sequel called *The Next Chapter*. I have received trophies and honors for serving my community and culture, but as a young gay Afro-American, I am still learning how to survive in a world of shame. I hope to graduate from college in 2000 or 2001.

The Dark Child

Cries of "Mommy, Mommy" whisper
in the air.
While me and my brother watch George Bush
make his famous speech about bombing
the Iraqis.
Eating leftovers from yesterday and the day
before that, Rice Krispies.
Guess what I found? A frozen chicken that
was in the freezer for months. The words on
the box said "Sell by November 15, 1991."
I throw it away.
Maybe I'll wait until Mommy comes home from cleaning
the white man's
house.

Mario Anthony Balcita, 21
San Francisco, Calif.

...and I was born. Into a life of old and had to grow up fast. San Francisco is home, no matter where I am. I don't remember how I became the muse I call myself, but I remember the steps. I found my voice in the Negro Spiritual Choir in second grade. I was "the" Mexican boy in front. Later I found my voice on the stage...in front...making the audience feel, express. Then I discovered I was gay—political by nature. I felt a voice, deep this time, and I learned to sing on paper and act with my pen. I discovered movement that I expressed in life. The beauty I have, no one can touch. I am a muse for the movement. So look for me in the sunset. These have been my first 21 years, and I await the next.

How I got here & where I'm goin'
a performance piece

If you could see it through my eyes,
you would understand why I'm blue in the face,
red on my feet,
and green everywhere in between.

Look
see me
and my mother
and her mother and father before me

With signs of hate!
Remember, "no dogs or mexicans allowed"?
My grandmother plowed picked and pulled,
to keep your bellies full
of the "american dream."

Though it seemed,
she got by with lighter skin...
...the american dream did my cookie-colored grandfather in.
They tried to bate and beat the system with dreams...
...Dreams is where their children would come from.

But mi abuelito couldn't cope,
for he long prayed and hoped for New Mexico to be old again,
escaping through clear glass bottles and tart breaths of heaven

Passed on to my mother was a life soaked in gin,
which she sifted through needles and bloodcells and tracks.

Look back at my eight-year-old father when his mother died.
She tried, but the only thing he inherited was her addictive trait.
His father fought for our country to free people from camps,
But wait!
Didn't our country have camps like that
for the Japanese or anyone who looked Asian?
They led my Filipino grandfather to believe he was leading a
freedom invasion...
...in my thoughts
He should have been home
fighting for love,
teaching my grandfather to love his son.

But the cruel fates have told him time is almost up,
for my father is dying inside,
from needles and bloodcells and medications.

Then there's the implications
his tracks I will trace.
I am not free to love or kiss or touch
look at my face, it betrays me, and my love is considered a sin.
I am not one or the other or both.
I am not going to let the american dream categorize me.
I am going to love whoever I want and
remember the hopes and dreams and hate and struggle that
came before me.

So throw your words...hate!
Your faggot, punk, nigger, bitch.
Your FOB, wetback, queer, spic.

Your breeder, dyke, honky, tramp.
Your 209 and 187,
we can't forget that.

You need to find some better way to attack,
cause let me tell you something
this fat boy gonna fight!
So you better stay the hell back!

And these are only a few things I have to carry.
So understand why I stand before you
with a tear on my face, a stain on my hand and the whiteness
taking over.

Rachel Josloff, 20
Long Island, N.Y.

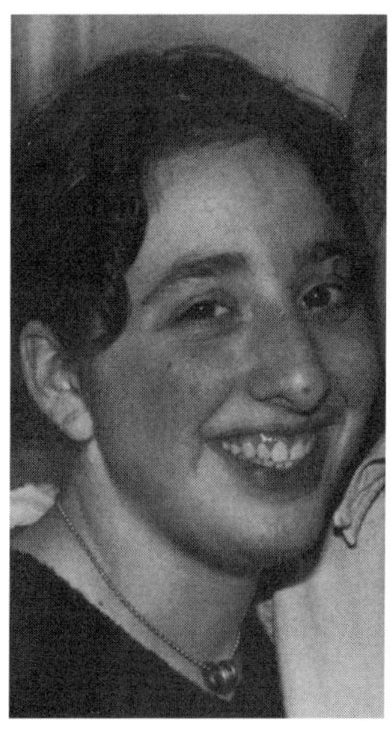

An art education major, I teach art to 5- to 17-year-olds on the weekends in central New York State. I'm in education because I believe children are the present, not the future, and that they should have as much of a voice as anyone else. I'm originally from Long Island, New York, and recently came out to my parents. Queer and feminist issues have played a prominent role in my work, and I think art is a starting point for enabling social change.

Untitled, pencil and crayon on paper, 8" x 11", 1998

Sherisse Alvarez, 17
Union City, N.J.

Audre Lorde says, "Poetry is not a luxury." It is a necessity, and I believe this is true for many artists and writers. As a writer and photographer, my work has its own language. Though I make a decision to write a poem or take a picture, my work is often involuntary, borne of a need to speak/create my own language. It addresses issues such as fragmentation, invisibility, and intimacy. As a 17-year-old queer Latina living between homes in New Jersey and California, I try to consciously work within the physical as well as the spiritual, attempting to find balance.

Line

There's a fine line between
what's right and what's wrong
Seconds.
Breaths.
It's funny how
one minute
you can be loving
then fucking
then cutting
each other with words that
seem to burn the tongue
Words you once whispered
to your sweetheart
your chula
your bitch
Your voice increasing
with each anger with each
raise of the hand with each
memory of childhood
The father who
was mostly violent
the mother always silent
Now it is your turn
to let it out
with the voice
with the fist
with the bitch who is your woman
Please Please Ay Please La Niña Is Watching

As you jam your dick deeper into her
as if wanting to eliminate
all the women
in the world
They are all the same
Puta.
Whore.
The place from where you emerged
now bleeding, split
as if just having birthed

reate.

dani frances montgomery, 20
Tucson, Ariz., and
San Diego, Calif.

I am a 20-year-old Irish/Algonkin/Scottish/French/etc. queer poet and activist. I grew up in Arizona and Southern California and now live in Northern California with my partner, Tracy. I write to celebrate where I come from and what I love as well as to speak about what makes me angry. I am trying to figure out what it means to be a college-educated high-school dropout femme-ish queer girl from a white working-class background, who was labeled "mentally ill" at a young age. I write to tell my own complicated truths, and I listen well to other people's. I teach with June Jordan's Poetry for the People program and Upward Bound, and I'm also an MFA student in creative writing at Mills College in Oakland, Calif.

dani frances montgomery

crazy girl: a reconstructed memory in three pieces

1.
still some nights
i hear the screams
of the six-year-old
strapped down in solitary
a sweet boy
so quiet in the day he
sat like a shell-shocked survivor
of some private war
staring at the gray pages
of his coloring book
while the older kids
talked about suicide, acid, and math

but between bed checks
his screams came through
the soundproof door
and we woke up
in the darkness
sweating our hospital beds
scared the nurses
might come next
for us

2.
when the door sticks
i panic
back to that 10 by 12 cubicle
where the nurse with hard eyes said

strip
so she could check
for drug stashes
inside my underwear
and the toes of my shoes
make sure i hadn't
hid a spray can in my pant leg or
strapped explosives on my stomach
and i sat naked on the coarse carpet
of the psych ward
as she clipped an i.d. tag
tight around my wrist

3.
monday
mandatory swim day
even in february
daniela offers me half her cigarette
as we sit shivering in the showers
with their cracked tiles and slime
tells me her father beat her
every night so finally
she drank a can of lighter fluid.
when she came out of her coma
the doctor prescribed prozac and
sent her to psych

out in the three-foot pool
attendants stand at the sides
tell us to keep moving
around and around
when Jason stops and

stands glaring
they remind him he can
go back to juvie if he won't behave

that afternoon my social worker
teaches me to play hearts
says it's a social skill that will
help me grab a boyfriend—
help me get
better

we would herd them together
the doctors scratching
prescriptions on yellow pads
the nurses with their needles
all the attendants, social workers
lock them in solitary
but we
don't have
the keys

the secret

look
here under my skin
you can see ireland's coast
a ribbon of green
disappearing behind
and up ahead the coal mines
of england / america
up ahead
the starched white servant's cotton
the railroad steel
glinting in yuma sun
the heavy kentucky air pressing
down on shoulders in the field
parish registers recording
catholic births
catholic deaths
names that sound
like ireland

look under my skin
here is the history lesson where
the french trapper takes a native bride
and her children
watch the line of green trees that braced the sky
recede under the push of new york steel and concrete
watch the tribe disappear behind her eyes
become a secret
whispered through generations
until we forget even
what the sound of it means

i sing with the rhythm
of lost islands and forgotten tribes
listen to my grandfather's new york
clanging behind my teeth
listen to my grandmother's footsteps
fading away in my heartbeat
listen
i am the secret
singing my own name over and over
imagining it will one day open up
and spill out an answer

sts, 25
Portland, Ore.

I write the 'zines *Nightmare Girl, Painter Lewis,* and *Way Down Low*. I also play drums with the Lookers, a Portland, Ore., dyke-pop band, with Sarah and Allison. Our first record is out on Candy Ass Records. I've made three short videos. The latest—and the only one I really like—is called "billy," and it's about how I deal with sexual abuse. Mostly I write and read personal narratives, my favorites being the 'zine *Doris*, *Annzine*, and the autobiography of Emma Goldman. Write me for 'zines: P.O. Box 40821, Portland, OR 97240.

exorcisms work when a person believes you are possessed and s/he is the person to deliver you. success is determined by the xtians' abilities to identify the demon by name + place a thick brick wall between you + the sin. the wall is **jesus christ**, and once he's there he's not supposed to be able to move. you go from one place of involuntary sin caused by the demon to the desired place of god's perfect love + protection.

this is how an exorcism feels:

helpless cause they won't let you leave or defend yourself. angry they aren't listening + can't understand, it hurts cause you're all stressed, tense, probably yelling or screaming + throwing stuff + hitting people. confused cause this is **you.**

once lesbianism was cast out of me, i felt like i had a new chance at avoiding hell. i had a clean slate + though rbyrd was nearby in sanfransisco i kept my word + followed their advice: pray the faith prayer + the commitment to god affirmation every day for 6 months, do not continue interacting with rbyrd, including letters, pray every night for spiritual armor (a detailed passage in the new testament).

i did everything they told me to. i got crushes on make-me-straight boys, almost any boy I came accross in chico. i believed. this is important everyone, you included troy. I believed in the demon, god, hell, heaven, the truth, and then one day rbyrd found my apartment, showed up at 2Am after a show, + since my IVCF house mate didn't realize anything about rbyrd + I, she didn't think to tell troy, + her visit was kept mostly a secret.

i couldn't help but kiss her. later on i felt like i was in love with her. none of the make-me-straight crushes were coming through. this time i only told kristy. she was the only one i could trust even though she continued to think i might go to hell anyway.

she knew it was my battle that no one else could help with. troy asked me to lead a bible study + i accepted the chance to grow closer to god, to show god i loved him more than rbyrd so maybe he would love me back if i was good.

halfway through my first year as a leader, i was 21 + living in the dorms where i had my bible study. rbyrd, over the summer, had converted to xtianity. although she didn't feel like beingalesbian would send anyone to hell, she decided to cut off our sexual relations because they were psychologically bad for her. damn. i was just making plans to graduate + follow her, devote all my heart to her, and now she was abandoning ship.

i couldn't blame her, i had been trying to sink us for 2 years. she did what she had to do to save herself, beaten down by all my god talk, my abuse of us in the name of god, my faith in jesus killing us off until finally she broke away + i cried for weeks, i remained depressed for months.

Katherine Heather Grobman, 26
Delran, N.J.

Looking back at my first 26 years, it seems everything should have been so obvious. But instead everything was so confusing. It's like one day I was absent and everyone else was taught the crucial aspects of being a boy or girl. I would lie in bed at night practicing and rehearsing how to be a boy. One day in middle school, after being pushed around again, a principal tried to teach me to "stop crying" and to "be a man." Bullies, teachers, and others taught me the same thing: There was something terribly wrong with my feelings. I tried so hard to purge from myself every expression of emotion. Really I only needed to be taught one lesson; we do not need to *learn* to be ourselves, we just *are* ourselves. A year ago I transitioned; I no longer practice being a young man; I just am a young woman. Today I have wonderful friends and the most perfect partner. I am also a Ph.D. student in developmental psychology. Someday I hope to teach college students and study how children learn and grow.

Am I Happy?

Hi, Mom and Dad,

Maybe you don't know this, but I think about things we say after we get off the phone. When we leave on bad terms it bothers me. And although being overwhelmed by grad school is one reason I don't call often, another is that it almost always turns out negatively. Our last conversation was wonderful, but I still think about our other conversations. One question you keep asking me is, "Does transitioning make you happy?" This is impossibly difficult for me to answer. It's hard for me to answer because I feel that no matter what my answer is, it's going to hurt you. Over and over again it seems you take issues in my life personally; the more I reveal how bad things were in childhood, the more you seem to feel you did something wrong. I usually just try to say nothing or leave things vague. But that just seems to make you feel like there's no reason behind what I'm doing. I have no idea how to begin to express something like this to you. Do you know how much of my behavior in your presence is catered to how I feel you'll respond? But that is a never-ending absurdity, so I'm going to try to be completely honest about expressing this to you. Please don't feel guilty about anything, because I don't, and I haven't ever blamed you for anything.

The other reason I have trouble answering "Am I happy?" is that my emotions are difficult for me to grapple with. It's only been in the last two or three years that I've really regained my ability to feel anything. You mentioned having seen my Web site (www.genderweb.org/~katherine/) so I won't go on and on telling you about the past. I feel kind of bad that I didn't screen my posted autobiography for anything that might offend you. But since I'm trying to say things honestly now, that's probably the best autobiography of mine you could read. Instead of focusing on the past, I feel

I should try to describe my present.

I guess maybe you look at my transition and think there must be one concrete thing about it that makes me happy. But there just isn't one concrete thing. There really are no things. I don't care much about clothes or makeup or styling my hair or any of the other zillion possible concrete things I could probably do better. It's why I get so frustrated when you focus on these things. This isn't about concrete things; it's about abstract feelings.

I spent my childhood in pain and my adolescence in a desperate attempt not to feel pain. Now I can feel pain. I can feel sadness. But I can also feel happiness. I like myself more today than any other time in my life.

I can relate to people in a positive way unlike ever before. I feel a part of other people's lives. I care about people, and I'm passionate about life in a way that's profoundly different from the way I've lived my life until now. And I have more self-confidence today than ever.

I can even deal with conflict in a fundamentally better way. I'm more assertive today than ever. I can express my feelings in ways I never would or could have before. My advisor and I are in a big conflict now. Even though I haven't completely stopped being passive-aggressive I've directly confronted her about many aspects of our conflict. I'm not staying in this bad relationship. And that's a big accomplishment for me; I never was able to leave the pharmacy job despite how horribly I was treated. Day after day I was yelled at for anything imaginable, and I still couldn't quit that job. I had "friendship" after "friendship" that was really based on people taking advantage of me. I finally like myself, and that empowers me to stop other people from mistreating me.

It's hard for me to bring my feelings into focus. Perhaps the answer is that transitioning does not make me happy. Transitioning is what makes it possible for me to *find* happiness.

And I'm still searching, and I'm still growing.

I wish you could see me living life every day. I'm so much more alive than I ever have been. I feel a lot better about myself as I watch myself grow through another adolescence. I truly feel I'm growing into a self-confident, well-balanced, and competent young woman.

And when I think about everything I'm trying to bring into focus for you, I can honestly say I am happy with making the decision to transition. I am also very happy that you are so supportive of me even when you can't understand what I can't say. I love you very much!

Katie

Uchechi Kalu, 20
Nigeria and the United States

I am a 20-year-old Igbo woman from Nigeria. I have lived most of my life in places throughout the United States. I write because poetry serves as my language. Without poetry, I would have never found the words to tell my story. In my culture, women, especially young women, are not encouraged to express our needs, passions, and desires. My art is an offering to my family and others, and I hope it will communicate and celebrate my truths. I am trying to find my voice as a Black queer woman living in the United States. Our society tries to speak for us young folks, and it's about time we find and use our own voices.

uchechi kalu

Affirmation

I be the one
momma always say
watch out for
be the reason my parents send me
to modeling school
make me a lady
who don't never want nothing
but a man

I be the one
who catch myself
looking at long black braids
and smelling apple plum perfume and you
I be the one not always lusting
after the big boys with beer bellies or biceps
'cause I be the one who like to choose

be the one
who don't know
how to claim this song / afraid to write this poem
how do I / stop myself / from disappearing
when there ain't no word
to translate my kind of love
into the syllables that decorate grandma's tongue

be the one make momma glance away
when my sister and I
strut down the hall
like a parade of peacocks
wearing daddy's suits

be the one Congress try to legislate out of sight
'cause I just don't act right

I be the one
loving women / loving men
loving you / who love me
I be the one
and I can't put a certain face
to love
I can't negotiate the tender curve of your spine
into a certain body frame
or carefully constructed gender identity

I be the one
momma always say
watch out for
be the one God don't like
be the one have to sit through
daddy's Sunday school lesson
about Sodom and Gomorrah
and how the Almighty burns them
out of sight
when they just don't act right

I be the one
my parents want to act like a lady
who don't never want nothing
but a man

But I be the one
who be loving women / loving men
loving you /who love me

'cause I ain't never gonna let nobody
tell me
to live
without love

Tasting Home

for June Jordan

as twin babies
my sister and I
cross the Atlantic
say good-bye to our African coast
in igbo and english
until at two years old
our mouths dry up
like the desert
only cries of hunger
escape our lips
and no one knows why
so my mother lifts her eyes
to the sky
raises her hands
as if waiting for manna from heaven
to loosen her babies' tongues

the child psychologist
advises her to stick to one language
he says speaking igbo and english
confuses kids
and so my parents drop igbo

only whisper it behind closed doors
like a secret

so I speak english only
sometimes pressing my ears
against my mother's bedroom door
hoping I can hear something anything
I can say at igbo parties
so other teenage girls do not laugh

I speak english only
unable to slash the silence
of three thousand miles
answering my grandfather
hello, can you hear me?

I speak english only
until my feet touch the red earth
of my Nigerian village
where igbo words fill the rhythm of the air
and my lips dry up
my eyes can only stare
praying for God to loosen my tongue

Then my professor says
we should write poems in home language
she says igbo words should dance across paper
never stopping until the beat of the song ends
then words fall from my lips
through long distance phone calls
asking mom how to say
something anything

to end this eighteen-year drought
now
words fall from my tongue
like rain from the sky
and I am tasting home
for the first time

Meliza Bañales, 21
Los Angeles, Calif.

I am a fierce-femme-in-your-face-spoken-word poet. I have been writing poetry for a number of years and have been doing spoken word for seven years. I have published my work in a series of 'zines and journals and just finished my first spoken word album, *Beauty Queen*. I am a creative writing major at the University of California at Santa Cruz, a member of the Santa Cruz Slam Team, and a gay-Xicana activist.

There is only one aspect to truth:
there is no truth,
only stories.
—proverb from Brazilian literature

Mensajes

This is me speaking for my soul
because she is on vacation

in first grade
the white girls
pulled
her blond hair
washed the half-white roots
to the floor
of a black-faced playground
where they blackmailed
her
with the brownness of her daddy
"No! don't tell anyone—
por favor,
no les habla a mis amigas"

This is me speaking for my soul
because she is on vacation

in summer streets
two teenagers
took fists and crowbars
to her Mexican father
"Go back to where you

came from
you fucking wetback!
Go home
beaner!"

but her 'apa
was no beaner,
rather a pigeon
swinging the feathers
from his wings
into the dusk of other men's tantrums

they were spilling her father's blood
        spilling her ancestry
        spilling the beans

oh, yes,
they were spilling the beans—
I'm American

This is me speaking for my soul

she kisses the labios
of a lover
who's too female
    too macha
    too dark
to be seen with her

ivory piano keys
fall into the lover's cinnamon sticks
as they glide down the boulevards

of East Los
past the cholos and her esas
the ones she calls
'familia'

they sit upon a dirty beach
to witness
a sunset
ready to give birth to the evening

but they are two much
          too long
          too late
          too bad—

they don't love each other enough
to keep standing
when the smoke clears

This is me speaking for my

her name is Bañales
but said the wrong way in
inglés
it is "Bangles" or "Banangles" or "Banuls"
and in español
it is "Pañales" ("Diapers")

the school children laugh
because they don't have a
curse
for substitute teachers

or college professors
to trip upon in public

the white people laugh
because they don't believe
white skin can be called
aloud
by a foreign tongue

the Mexicans laugh
because they expect her
not to know the pun
but to smile,
                        have the husband
                        have the house
                        have the babies and
know how to change their underpants

This is me speaking for

she is a big white house
with brown furniture and
matching curtains

her body is bathed in dresses and lipstick
her lovers are bathed in neckties, three-piece suits, hidden
        breasts

she sings old church songs
her abuelita taught her
when she was the size of a small

rose bush
where in time,
she becomes the graceful flowers
bleeding thorns
drinking the lyrics of old women
as she grows
soft
into herself

she is the adobe stove house
baking tortillas
while knitting a kilt
mixing them together
to form one coat
                                        of
                                            arms

and no,
she does not have an ending for this
and yes,
this makes you uncomfortable
but life and the memory
can only keep the jaw
wired
for so long

This is me speaking

Speaking.

Kevin Rolfe, 26
Essex, Great Britain

Born in Dagenham, Essex, Great Britain, I am now a 26-year-old big, queer, cheeky, East-End yob! I started writing years ago after hearing the term "writing as therapy." Since then I've continued to write and have quite a bit published. I seem to be doing OK, getting gay-related poems published in straight-aimed anthologies and refusing to be ghettoized, pigeon-holed, or swept aside with all the other gay British writers. This poem is one of a series I have written about substance abuse.

Side Effects

I'm itching nearly everyday
At least a few days
a fortnight;
Wondering if I'm gonna wake up
with a scratch-covered face
red raw;
Take off my top
see the red lines
and add heaps more
Will my groin be bleeding?
Scabby in the morning
when I wake up;
But I haven't slept yet
I try
But the scratching.
Someone stop me.

Sara Frog Davidson, 20
Concord, Calif., and Boston, Mass.

My name is Sara Ann Davidson, but most people call me Frog. I paint things in books and on cardboard I find on the street. I draw angry bears that look like monkeys (maybe that's why they're angry) and bald kids that look sad. I go to the School of the Museum of Fine Arts, Boston. There are a lot of bricks in Boston.

My work has been described as dank and intimate and edgy and comforting. I think it's more like when you think you're losing your mind, but something brings you back, like an old photograph or a burrito-shop receipt. Or whatever, so it goes.

sara frog davidson

bruised, watercolor and crayon on found book, 16" x 11", 1997

Dana Nicole Robinson, 20
Compton, Calif.

I was raised in Compton, Calif., and am a writer, singer, dancer, and poet. I attend Santa Clara University, studying psychology and dance. I wish someone would have told me on my way out of the womb that life would not be an easy journey. We are not born into this world with a sense of our own identity, so we spend our lives searching for our own truths. Finding my truth has been one of the most challenging endeavors of my life.

In my journey toward truth I have discovered that many people refuse to accept my sexual identity as one that is not gender-specific. But this is my truth. And some people still refuse to embrace my identity as a strong Black woman. But this is also my truth.

Although adversity has been no stranger to me, I have been able to rise above it all. So I would like to express to today's queer youth that they need not conform to society's stereotypes, but instead find their own truth, wherever it may be.

Never Too Good at Dressing Barbies

This morning my love, I know that I
love you. You called for me for what
seemed like the thousandth time this
hour. My frustration brought to a halt
when I saw you kneeling over the john.
I stayed bent on the floor with you as
your meals reversed their flow.

Clenching your stomach from behind is
not like it used to be. Your bones, no
longer hidden by the dressings of
skin. Face, hollowed out and narrow.
Skin, consumed by unexpected sores.
Your strong runner's legs now resemble
fragile twigs ready to break in the wind.
And your voice, it doesn't echo with
seduction anymore, instead it is the color
of shame, regret and fear. While you slide
on your bra, I see that your breasts have
forgotten how to overflow in my cupped
hands. Nipples turned inward. Your
entire body asking me in silence if I still
love you. YES.

Holding in my tears I say, "Forgive me if
I am too rough. I was never too good at
dressing Barbies." You smile until the
pain demands you stop.

Laura, 16
Pennsylvania

I attend a Catholic all-girls school in Pennsylvania. I am active in a lot of school activities but believe writing is the most effective way to express myself. Lauren is my girlfriend of nine months.

Lauren, 16
Pennsylvania

I am a dyke. I originally came out as bi, but through my relationship with Laura I have realized I only want to be with girls. It's my natural way of living, and though my parents aren't accepting of it, I continue to act on what I believe in and what my heart tells me is right. I go to the same all-girls Catholic school as Laura. Because of this, I'm not too open at school about being a dyke, but I use writing as a means of expressing an identity I cannot speak.

Poems whispered in the dark by Laura and Lauren, to each other

Glow Worm
by Lauren

when our lips are touching
a waterfall of her warm breath
seeps down in between our mouths
that is the purest air i ever inhaled

Untitled
by Laura

in the dim light of my room
after the footsteps have stopped
i sink into you
i bare my body to your eyes
the same body i conceal from the world
your eyes peruse my curves and accept them
only you love my flaws
the heat between our bodies burns my flesh
melts away insecurity
under the covers your fingers perfect my naked body
your skin clothes me
i hover above you and watch you watch me move
your eyes give me strength
your breath—reassurance
in the dim light of my room
after the footsteps have stopped
i accept myself

Anna Mills, 23
Palo Alto, Calif.

I am a 23-year-old lesbian feminist currently working for Americorps in an inner city school. I majored in English at Williams College and dream of teaching writing for social change. Mostly I write about body image and sexuality and have given workshops on queer women's body image at the Models of Pride conference in Los Angeles and at the Young Women's Health Fair in San Francisco.

Secret Hungers

I had an eating disorder in high school. Like millions of American girls, I hated my body. I ate compulsively, and believed I could never be normal. I was achingly envious of thin, attractive women.

I sat hunched over my books, eating piece after piece of buttered toast, unable to taste the bread. I lay down with an aching stomach, feeling the extra folds of skin, the soft flesh. I got up to run for miles, my legs pounding, determined to be clean. At school I watched a fellow actress in the dressing room as she posed in her black lingerie costume. Her slim curves, her long blond hair, the silk straps over her tan skin. Unreachable beauty.

I was fascinated when men liked me. I believed that by controlling my weight, I could ensure a boyfriend's loyalty. If he drifted away, I knew he had finally noticed my body was too big. If he stayed, I was hungry for sex. His desire made me feel alive. I couldn't name my own needs or desires, much less assert them. I could not touch him unless he touched me. Part of me stayed numb while we kissed for hours. Sometimes I felt waves of sickness. Sometimes I was drawn into passion like a whirlpool in darkness. Through all this, I was positive of one thing: One day I would lose the weight and begin to glow.

As my eating obsession raged on in college, feminist accounts of eating disorders reassured me. I was suffering from issues of body image and sense of self that affect all women in our society. Because women are treated as sex objects, I learned, we are often alienated from our sexuality and from our desires. That made sense to me. I knew there was something wrong with the way I kept sneaking and stealing food, eating boxes of cookies at a time and hating myself. But I also knew there was something deeply wrong with my passive, fearful sexuality. I latched onto feminist writers as my liberation.

I used all the tools I could find to develop my sense of self and my ability to communicate. I learned to speak, through therapy, support groups, writing stories, in journals, arguing in classes, talking for hours on the phone—desperately trying to connect to others, to understand my feelings and needs and make myself heard. I learned that I wanted to be big, to take up space, to rage. I slowly began to transform my hunger into language.

* * *

Throughout the process of recovery, I never questioned my sexuality. Lesbians were the "Other," and the idea of wanting a woman was an empty space. It amazes me that my imagination was so controlled by my culture that I could not recognize something so central to my being. But the long process of learning to speak and learning to take up space had prepared me.

Something shifted inside me. Something light, crazy, and joyous took hold of me. I felt like I was dancing through my life. I came out, and it was as if a heavy, dark cloud had been lifted from me. A happiness I had only glimpsed before was now possible. I stared at women on the street, in my classes, in movies.

And I noticed a strange correlation. I still felt an electric response to women's bodies. Now, however, I named it differently. Instead of envy and despair, it was a flash of heat and recognition. "She's so sexy," I would whisper, then hug myself and smile.

The change was dizzying. I came out to friends, family, and to my whole campus in the span of two weeks. The threat of my eating obsession disappeared. It would never return.

I had prayed for years for someone to tell me, plainly and simply, what my eating disorder was about. No theory suggested that shame about my body, my needs, and desires might be shame about my queer sexuality. None suggested that envy of women might be a cover for desire. Those suggestions may be too threatening to straight feminists. Most women suffer from similar anxiety, guilt, and food obsession, and all women are constrained by compulsory heterosexuality. Perhaps food and body-image obsession are a secret language for all women. They speak a rebellion, a refusal to fit mind and soul into the role of the perfect straight girl. They speak women's hunger for more intimate, physical, primary relationships to other women. Their rebellion is silent—it draws attention to the symptom and not the cause.

As I came out, I began to feel that my body belonged to me. I stopped scrutinizing it for ugliness or sexiness. I stopped feeling like an object, and more like a body in relation to other women's bodies. When I talked with a woman I was attracted to, I could feel the energy in me and between us, in our words, our postures, our smiles—a link across empty space. I developed innumerable tiny crushes. I'd had crushes when I was straight, but they made me feel inadequate and wistful. With my new crushes, I didn't stop to worry about measuring up. I prized my feelings and talked about the crush as if it were an accomplishment.

My residual feelings of guilt about eating evaporated. I would still sit down and eat a box of cookies at a stretch fairly frequently. But I usually let myself shrug off the complex, painful emotions that go with a binge. They seemed like a waste of energy. The guilt and secrecy were unnecessary.

I began to take pride in the fact that I would never be the perfect, pretty, docile straight girl—treasured by my family and by men, celebrated by society. As a young white woman in a racist society, I grew up with this fantasy of white womanhood—that I was to be cherished, protected and admired. I lived in a rich, white suburb where I was cushioned by privilege. We never talked about the neighboring town of people of color; we knew very few people who lived there. Yet we believed we were progressive and pro civil rights. I was blind to the racism around me and inside me, just as I was to the homophobia and sexism.

I am just beginning to understand how my whiteness affected my eating disorder and my gender role. I am just beginning to see how I can fight not just my own oppression, but also other kinds of blindness and hate.

I may never be that "perfect" girl, but I know I am someone much stronger and happier—a woman-loving baby dyke. Not diseased by homophobia, but coming into my own, coming out of my nightmare cocoon.

Daryl Vocat, 23
Regina, Saskatchewan

I am 23 and have lived in Regina all my life. Soon I will be moving to Toronto, where I will be working on my master's degree in fine arts. I have been involved in several art shows and exhibitions over the past few years and have also had a considerable amount of my writing published in various punk rock 'zines as well as newsletters and other independent media. I got involved in activism through punk rock music and the community I found there.

I have a difficult time defining myself in terms of sexuality, so I often use the term *queer* to describe myself. I use it as a celebration of sex and sexual diversity. I am attracted to people, not just one particular sex, gender, or race. I like to think my capacity to relate to people and create meaningful relationships goes beyond our differences and gets to the core level of humanity.

Tug of War Grip, etching, 38 x 35.5 cm, 1999

A Process of Change, etching, 38 x 35.5 cm, 1999

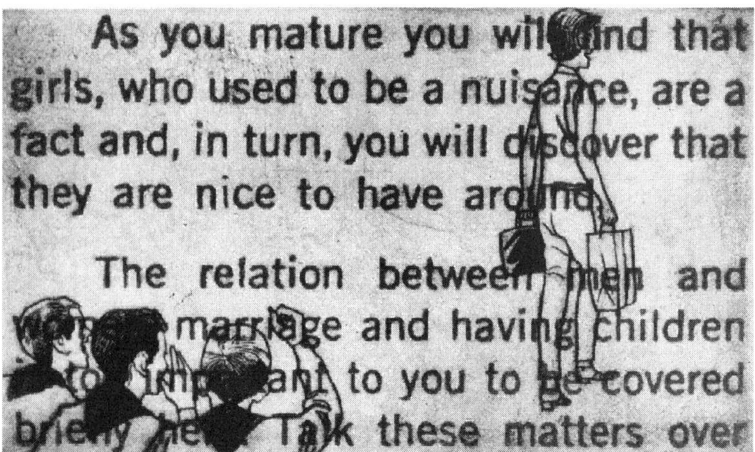

A Healthy Attitude, etching, 38 x 35.5 cm, 1999

The Promise, etching, 38 x 35.5 cm, 1999

Kohei Ishihara, 19

I am a gay biracial (Japanese and white), Nissei, male, genderqueer. I spent four years abroad (two years in Nepal and two years in Japan) before attending high school in Bethesda, Md. My life pursuits are in HIV/AIDS, cultural, and queer activism (and most of the time, a combination of all three). I am a sophomore at Brown University, majoring in ethnic studies and sexuality & society.

Piecing Together My Racial Identity

Race and racial identification have always been confusing concepts for me. What is my ethnicity? What do I look like? What do other people think I am? These questions baffled me throughout my childhood, growing up in a white, upper-class, suburban neighborhood. My elementary school told me who I was. My teacher told me to hold the Japanese flag to celebrate the international diversity of our class. Dustin Chow, who held the Chinese flag, was the only other Asian kid in the class. He pointed to me one day and told me that my eyes were slanted. But sometimes my eyes did not look slanted. And neither did Dustin's. I think that white people sometimes get confused and say that small, beautiful eyes are slanted. My middle school told me who I should be. My phys ed. teacher was amazed that I was half Japanese. He said, "Wow, you really don't look Japanese at all. You look white." He smiled. Perhaps he was hitting on me. But nevertheless, he was telling me that I looked white, and he meant it as a compliment. So I tried to become white. But I just did not fit in with the other white guys. I could not compare myself to them. And they always made sure I knew that I was different. "Kohei, you have black hair, not brown hair."

I angrily spoke back, "No, look at my hair. It's dark brown, not black."

"No, it's black," they said. In relation to their eyes and hair, my eyes became slanted and my hair became black.

There were no Asians in my high school. Ravinder was half Asian, but because his other half was Black, he said he considered himself Black. Black, white, yellow...I was actually unconcerned about my racial identity. I wanted to come *out.* I wanted to meet Queer people. But there were no Queer people in my high school. Perhaps there were, but they were in the closet like me.

And perhaps there were other biracial Asians who passed as white or Black, like Ravinder and I. After I came out to several friends, I finally decided: I wanted to claim my identity as Asian. So on my SATs I checked off "Asian/Pacific Islander."

Now I'm out to my parents, family, friends, and foes. I have joined many different Queer and Asian Pacific American (APA) organizations. I also have become an AIDS activist, and I pass out condoms to people of color. As I walk through the streets doing this, I look for people of color, but sometimes it is difficult to tell whether one is of color. When I'm only supposed to pass them out to APAs, it becomes even more difficult.

"Is he Filipino? Wait, he might be Latino."

"Is that girl APA, because she might be a mix between Russian and ethnic-Jewish."

When I accidentally assume someone's ethnicity I feel embarrassed. But it happens a lot. I've been assumed Asian, European, Latino, native Hawaiian, and Nepali! I find it fascinating when someone assumes my racial identity. I often ask them why and what characteristics or features led them to make that assumption. Just the same, being outgoing me in my tight shirt and trendy eyebrow ring leads many people to think I am gay. And I am. But for many people, their only images of gay people are whites—like on *Will & Grace*. Basically, people know little about race, racial identity, ethnicity, geographic origin, religion, and color. These terms are often used interchangeably. My racial identity is (yes, I've finally made up my mind!) APA and white. I'm not Asian because I grew up in the United States and so prefer to be called Asian Pacific American. I use the word *Pacific* not because I'm a Pacific Islander, but because Pacific Islanders, East Asians, Southeast Asians, and South Asians have all been lumped together in the United States. APAs come from more than 40 different nationalities and speak more than 100 different languages.

We are brown, yellow, black, white, and everything in between. We have small eyes, large eyes, big noses, flat noses, curly hair, and straight hair. But for some reason we are all labeled "Asian/Pacific Islanders."

Even if we don't have the language to distinguish ourselves, our government should at least stop treating us like foreigners. We have been in the United States since the 1800s and we are still not called Asian Pacific *Americans*. But the government plans to change this category for the next census. They plan to separate Pacific Islanders from Asian Americans. Perhaps in the future they will mix us around again. But amidst all of Hollywood's negative or exoticized images of us and the racist threats, name-callings, and arbitrary governmental classifications, I know who I am. I stand firmly as an Asian Pacific American. Though I am not South Asian or Pacific Islander, I still consider them my brothers and sisters. It's sort of like taking the government's hasty classification of us and using it to our advantage, to empower us as a unified people. Perhaps one day they will feel threatened by our collectivity and try to racially divide us. See how flimsy, fluid, and confusing race can be? Like my gender (male genderqueer), sexuality (gay) and economic status (upper middle class), my race (biracial APA and white) is a socially constructed identity. We tend to view race and identity as a whole, as something that is fixed and stable. Well, honey, I've been transracial and fluid my whole goddamn life! As the slogan goes, "Race is Fiction, Racism is Real."

Alix Lindsey Olson, 23
Bethlehem, Penn. and Brooklyn, N.Y.

Originally from southeast Pennsylvania, I live in Brooklyn with my homemade, handmade feminist family. We have discovered that art is only universal if you are a male artist speaking to men. We work to create art that speaks to women's experiences through cartooning, photography, acting, and poetry.

The Nuyorican Poets Cafe has been my other family, a home in which political spoken word is highly valued. We won the National Slam Championships this year and appear on a new CD called *Unbound,* a spoken-word compilation benefiting political prisoner Mumia Abu-Jamal. I've had the opportunity to perform at a diverse range of venues, such as Harlem's Apollo Theatre, the 1998 Gay Games in Amsterdam, Labor Party Conferences, and a number of queer rallies and political marches.

I've found that art is one of the most powerful ways to spread word about political realities. Speaking to each other about our individual truths will begin to unravel this mess. The rest is up to us to create.

Private Anniversary With Mom was written in collaboration with Jessica Arndt, a student at Wesleyan University and a self-described pirate dyke/feminist/writer/kid.

Private Anniversary With Mom Or, On Coming Home With Short Hair

Written With Jessica Arndt

Four years ago today
“Are you sure you’re a...” the word
plump and silent between us,
like a red rubber dodge ball.
“I should have had men around,” she says.
“Did *I* buy you Audre Lorde?”
her eyes are wired to will me into a woman:
“It’s hard, you know, the lifestyle,”
thinking maybe she can make the world
balance her blame.
Four years ago today
she comes at me,
a new solution slipping from her teeth,
soggy with hope — “aha!” she cries.
“*They* wear combat boots,
and you’ve always been a sneaker girl.”
Four years ago today
and I still don’t say
that when we make love,
we do it with our shoes off.

America’s on Sale!

ATTENTION SHOPPERS!!!
attention 9 to 5 folk, cell-phone masses.
the “up-and-coming” classes
Attention sport-utility,

plastic-surgery suburbanites,
viagra-popping, gucci-shopping urbanites
Attention george clooney-loonies,
promise-keeper sheep,
stockbroker sleepwalkers,
big investment talkers,
ricki lake watchers
Attention walmart congregation,
shop-'til-you-drop generation,
ATTENTION NATION!
AMERICA'S ON SALE!

We've unstocked the welfare pantry
to restock the wall street gentry
It's economically elementary,
'cause values don't pay
Yes, american dreams are on permanent layaway,
(*'cause there was limited availability anyway*)
So the statue of liberty's being dismantled,
$10 a piece to sit on your mantle
or hang on your wall by the small somalian child
you bought from sally struthers
sisters and brothers, it's now or never,
these deals won't last forever—
AMERICA'S ON SALE!
restrictions may apply if you're Black, gay, or female.

And shoppers,
global perspective is 99% off
'cause most of the world don't count to us
Our ethnic inventory's low
'cause moral business has been slow,

Yes, the values-company is moving to mexico—
and ALL ETHICS MUST GO!

National health care's 100% off!!
and medicare's in the 50% bin,
so you can buy half an operation
when AMERICA'S ON SALE!
And there's a close-out bid to determine
which religion will win
all the neon flashing signs of sin say
the christian coalition is bidding high
shoppers, you ask WHY?
who needs a higher power when you've got
purchasing power
to corner and market
one human mold
that's right—real family values are being UNDERSOLD!

and it's open hunting season for the NRA!
so there's a special uzi discount—only today!
Gun control? we say—
black bear, black man, blow 'em both away!
and the Guiliani welfare mamas are on the auction block
again, we're closing out this country the way we began.
so step up for our fastest selling commodity
no waiting lines for HIV,
condoms and needle exchange are a hard to sell thing
(to the right wing)
so if you're a druggie or a fag—
rent-to-own your own body bag NOW!
WHILE AMERICA'S ON SALE!

we're selling fast to the AT&T CEO,
he's stealing all utilities, he doesn't pass go,
and collect $1,000,000 anyway.
He's the monopoly winner
'cause he bought the whole board
and we bought the whole game
now no price is the same!
'cause inflation's up on the CEO ego
and power's deflated as far as we go:
'cause nike bought the revolution
and law schools bought the constitution
and tommy hilfiger bought red, white, and blue
a flag shirt for fifty dollars,
the one who's being burned is you!
marlboro bought what it means to be a man
and lexus equals power—get it while you can
and maybelline bought beauty,
and new york's buying rudy
and mastercard gold's sought the national soul
broadway bought talent and called it *CATS*!
the republicans bought out the democrats
they liquidated all asses in a fat white donkey sale—
now it's buy one shmuck, get one shmuck free
in the capitalist party!
and there's nothing left to get in the way
of a full blue-light blowout
of the US of A!

there's a no-nothing back guarantee,
a zero-year warranty
when you buy this land of the fritos, ruffles, and lays...
this home of the braves and the reds and the slaves!

so call 1-800-i don't care about shit
or www.FUCK ALL OF IT
to receive your credit for the fate of our nation—
interest is at an all-time low

so with these sales-pitching verses
i should win for customer service
i'm like CRAZY EDDIE—
i'm GOING INSANE IN AMERICA!
where the almighty dollars sparkle and shine,
this Star Bucks Land that's yours and mine.
but america's selling fast shoppers.
BUY IT WHILE YOU CAN!
'cause america's been downsized, citizens

and you're all fired.

Beth Ann Dowler, 19
Batesville, Ark., and Norwich, Conn.

Born in Arkansas, I was partially raised by strict Southern Baptist grandparents. Religion is often a huge part of Southern life, and unfortunately for most queer youth, it can also be a huge barrier between they and their families.

On Christmas day 1996 I came out to my grandparents. Sticking to their strict Southern Baptist doctrine, they rejected me and we haven't spoken since. This story is written in the hope that some parent, grandparent, uncle, aunt, or sibling out there will read it and consider the pain rejection causes before turning their backs. Although this story is fiction, it is based on actual events.

Currently I reside in Norwich, Conn., with my fiancée, Kris Wiedenheft. I would like to thank my mom, Arkansas School for Math and Sciences, and my teacher, Dr. Keith Hale, for helping me survive and be where I am today.

Washed in the Blood

I straightened my skirt and snuck into the back of the church. 11:15. That meant the preacher was already raining his usual torrent of hellfire and damnation threats onto his dwindling congregation. The population had been decreasing for as long as I could remember. The trend appeared unchanged as I noted about 15 or so people and tried to conceal myself in the back pew.

"...and the sinners of this world WILL BE TRIED AT THE HAND OF GOD ALMIGHTY HIMSELF..."

Just as I'd guessed. When I was younger I used to think every word was directed toward me. Even at 4 or 5 I would hear those angry words and know, somehow, that God must hate me. That I was bad—for whatever reason. That if I didn't do exactly as I was told I most certainly would go to hell—and that was bad.

"...let us pray, Dear Lord..."

That was how it always started. Every young child is taught well by doting grandmothers and pious parents, "Bow your head, darling, close your eyes."

"*Jesus loves the little children / all the children of the world / red and yellow, black and white / they are precious in his sight / Jesus loves the little children of the world.*"

I was 4, maybe 5, when I learned all the words. It wasn't until 11 or 12 that I realized: Jesus may love them, but I'm not supposed to. The church I'd gone to was all white. The churches I'd visited were all white. Even the camp we attended had only a token minority or two, and even then, they were never Black.

"...Please turn in your Bibles to..."

I was "saved" at 7—from what I didn't really understand. I just knew it was a bad thing to *not* be "saved" and that everyone wept for joy at my timid question, "How can I be saved?"

It was my grandmother who planned everything—what I wore, what I ate, who came, etc. She was the one who stood proudly beside me forcing me to take congratulatory handshakes and shedding the compulsory "tears of joy." The church gave me a Bible, King James version. The preacher had it stamped with my name—my badge of Christendom, so to speak.

"...to Ephesians 5:22-33..."

I looked at the faded blue cover and thought about all the trouble that little book had caused. Hundreds of wars killing millions of people. The persecution of Jews, homosexuals, Blacks, Latinos, Native Americans, Arabs, Asians, women, and hundreds of innocent "heathen" civilizations. All because one large group of people claimed they were more right than anyone else in the world.

"...Wives, submit yourselves unto your own husbands..."

I had to beg my wife, Julie, to let me come alone today. "I need to do this," I begged over and over. "Why? This is crazy!" she said. Maybe it was. Maybe not. But I just kept thinking that maybe, just maybe, I still had a chance.

The last three years had been the hardest of my short life. Both of us in college now and well on our way to spending the rest of our lives together. Far away from those who'd exiled me, I'd found safety on the East Coast with my wife. There I could hide in the oceans of wonderful, colorful people. Still, the little Southern girl inside me couldn't forget—something I hoped to resolve in that small white country church.

"...let us pray..."

She was looking at me. The ancient matriarch I'd come to confront was looking. I could feel it. I hadn't been paying attention; I was so lost in memories. I glanced up, a smile fluttering around the corners of my mouth. She turned away.

White as a ghost, I knew she recognized me, but every inch of her presence said it *did not, would not* acknowledge me. I wanted to scream and cry. I wanted to shout, "I am a lesbian. I am happy. *Why* can't you accept that?" But I didn't.

I quietly got up and slipped out of my pew. The rest of my world could never be the same. My faith was dying.

As I closed the age-worn door behind me, I heard the preacher dismiss the congregation. I knew that in her silence I was supposed to find dismissal as well. She had already gone back to her safe little world. She was protected from me by her belief in a cruel "God" that uses disease as a punishment for sinners. Where loving someone only means praying for them when you can't accept the things they do. Where, out of fear, people don't mix with "different" kinds of people.

As for me, I got into my car and went back to my wife.

Matt Wiedenheft, 15
Norwich, Conn.

I reside in Norwich, Conn., and am a fine arts student. I enjoy skating, art, Swedish fish, and coffee.

Broken, mixed media, 28" h, 1998

De Anne Lyn Smith, 21
Endicott, N.Y.

Born and raised in upstate N.Y., I now live in Alfred, N.Y., where I spend my time writing poetry, short fiction, essays, letters, postcards, requests for funds for our local women's group, ridiculously boring press releases, illegible notes on everything from memoir to early medieval European history, and words in the sky.

de anne lyn smith

Further Falling

Self pressed to self, breast reflects breast
as we tense, shedding senses,
pushing our muscled tongues to the edge

of death. Lover, if each touch
is a step to hell, then let
me celebrate your devil neck,

your cleft toes, the red swell
of flesh where you have bled.
Let me ascend the steps

of your breathing; lead me,
please, through this deep evening.
Dear, we must be heathens,

our clean bare feet creasing
sheets as we heat pieces
of dreams in these free flames.

We believe in release.

Tim Arevalo, 19

A child of Ibalon, now living in the Diaspora, I am a queer Pilipino poet who has called Manila and Pasay City, Philippines, as well as Oakland, Daly City, and San Francisco, Calif., home. I was the 1998 Teen Poetry Slam Champion in San Francisco and a member of the San Francisco team for the National Teen Slam in Albuquerque, N.M. Anxiously waiting, I am heading off to New York to attend Eugene Lange College this fall and am considering ways to fuse creative writing and public health in my undergraduate studies. I will be taking donations, because I will be sorely in debt after tuition payments. *Mabuhay ang rebolusyon!*

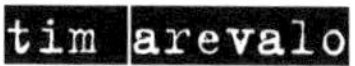

a poem for us

if believing in Gods were still so simple
might I ask,
what God was it that plucked us
from heaven's branches
sewed us into our mothers' wombs
to sprout for us
to blossom for us
to be beautiful for us?

What God was it that slid us onto this planet
as slick as we are
with lightning for tongues
and gave us the task of poets?

I don't care anymore, it hurts too much to think of it
so I don't concern myself with such things
it's all irrelevant now, because

we are nothing less than great
but that's too much to believe, isn't it?

we've got to stay comfortable hating ourselves
seeing hideous monsters in our reflections
so we can keep trying to escape these ugly bodies
because hurting this bad is the only way we know we are still
alive

we are nothing less than great
but this truth we dread, waving blazing fists in its face
clenching doubt in our tender palms

because we are too coward to love ourselves

how have we managed to travel so little
but hate ourselves so much

Ginsberg said he saw the best minds of his generation
destroyed
I have seen the same

I have seen us in our rooms
foil and lighter in our hands
straw in our lips and nose
chasing black dragons and snorting white cobras
because ten dollars was cheap
for a double hit of joy

I have seen us hunched over toilet bowls
vomiting self-esteem down the drain
because *Vogue* and *Elle* always
had beauty in a size 3 and that
was only a heave-ho and upchuck away

I have seen us on the corner
complacent and numb
copping doom in dime bags
because we didn't know that
the grim reaper wore Filas and a hoodie

I have seen us swigging
golden poison because we
were fooled and thought manhood
was sold in 40-ounce bottles

I have seen us spread our legs like the horizon
because some man tricked us into accepting
that love was only found on our backs

I have seen
us
I have seen
us

and I am not a coward anymore
star trekking through the universe
boldly going to the next   cosmic hit
                                        astral high
searching for stardust and moon rocks to get us by

I am not a coward anymore
I see us for what we are
nothing less than great, because
we are the poets

the derelict cats who prance on fine lines of chance
the sky rips open for us, luck lands on our laps
we confuse the wind, dismiss it
and send it off to all directions
we tap dance on the shoulders of waves
and give height to the tides
we walk and talk mountains
breathe hurricanes, hum earthquakes
and our kisses are wet haikus glistening on crimson pages

we are nothing less than great
more than divine

but great and divine are still just words
and words still have walls
and walls are nothing but limits
but we are limitless
so we are even beyond articulation

we are nothing less than great
the world is waiting, holding their breath, waiting for us
the poems are waiting, holding their breath, waiting for us
they are waiting for us
to speak our thunder
time is flying away on precious gilded wings
we cannot be cowards anymore
the stakes are too high
the poems are too many

the world is waiting for us
to claim the mountain tops
siphon the sun into our pens
and illuminate the page

on the mountains top
where we are Gods and Goddesses
and fear and hate are obsolete

just take my hand
there's nothing I can show you
you can't see for yourself
but just take my hand
if you too cannot believe we are cowards and victims
there's a universe for us to write about
and stars for us to conquer

let's start right here on this mountain top
where we are Gods and Goddesses
who do not know the meaning of defeat
take my hand, if you want
and let's write these poems together

Amy Sonnie, 22
Newtown, Penn.

I am a 22-year-old writer, editor, and activist from Pennsylvania. I identify as queer, a term I use to describe both my sexual and political identities as a bi/feminist/antiracist activist committed to revolutionary social change. I use writing—articles, poetry, essays—as a form of advocacy, as well as for self-healing. I am committed to working for racial, economic, and social justice.

Halloween 1997

for Malachi

they made you watch while they did it
so you'd never forget
her eyes glassy with fear, searching
your face for recognition as
five fists rain on her,
two guys hold you back, saying
"watch butch, watch"
aren't you supposed to save her

and after the thunder of laughter
the blood-stained concrete
the snap of bones and pride
you couldn't bring yourself
to look at her, couldn't live
with yourself reflected
helpless and beaten
in her eyes

but i want to tell you that you're strong
that i see you walking those same streets
one year later
wearing the same clothes
holding your head high
in order to say
i have survived
two years on the streets and
i have survived
deprogramming camp for queers and

i have survived
eighteen years
gang wars and ridicule
my father's fists, my mother's scorn
and

i have survived
have saved
myself
time and again
in order to say
i own myself
and no fist can pound that
out of me.

Ryn Gluckman, 20
Rutland, Vt.

I am a 20-year-old legal studies major at Hampshire College in Amherst, Mass. I spend my time playing pool, fencing, drinking too much coffee, and laughing loud and hard.

Relearning the Mothertongue: Notes From a Second-Generation Queer

I was ten when my mother asked if I knew what "homosexual" meant. We were sitting on the front porch in late April, just after all the snow had melted. The ground was wet and cold, still too full with winter for bare feet. But the sun was bright and warm on the back of my neck. I felt my mother looking at my face carefully. I could tell by the tone of her voice that she was about to have a Serious Conversation with me. Out of habit, my eyes slipped to the ground, back up to the sky, over to the trees, tracing imaginary bird flights, anywhere but her face. A Serious Conversation meant she was going to tell me something I didn't want to hear.

"Erin, do you know what 'homosexual' means?"

I shrugged, another standard for Serious Conversations. I didn't know what it meant, although I had some idea it was related to "homo," which had become one of the more popular fifth-grade taunts.

"So, you don't know what 'homosexual' means?"

Another shrug, eyes averted, though I knew she wanted me to look at her. I squinted, closed one eye, and the trees turned into green elephants.

She sighed and began to speak slowly, thinking about each word. "Homosexuality is when a woman loves a woman or a man loves a man, sort of like when a husband loves a wife or a girlfriend loves a boyfriend. When a woman is a homosexual she is a lesbian, when a man is homosexual he is gay." She was becoming a little more comfortable now. I fidgeted. I was becoming a little more nervous. "Do you understand, Erin?"

Shrug.

"So, when your father and I divorced, part of the reason was because I found out I was a lesbian."

I raised an eyebrow, a trick I had been working on for months. "Do you understand what that means, Erin?"

I kept my head down and considered this a long time before I spoke. Finally I mumbled, "Means you like girls."

* * *

I was 16 and had told no one I lived in a home with two mothers. I didn't invite people home from school. When my mother marched in a Halloween parade under the banner of a local gay and lesbian task force with a mask on her face, people threw eggs at her. I went to school the next day and laughed at the fag jokes. I was convinced that if people found out I would be beaten, mistaken for queer myself, graded lower, or sent into adolescent exile.

That spring, our town newspaper printed a letter to the editor written by Karol Jones, an enraged mother. She came home one day to find her son flipping through *Daddy's Roommate*, a kids' book found in the children's section of the public library. *Daddy's Roommate* is a picture book, written from the view of a 7-year-old boy who goes to visit his gay father and his father's lover. The book describes the things the boy and his two dads do with each other: fishing, eating, and talking. Karol was outraged that the library carried books "promoting abnormal lifestyles" in the children's section where just any "innocent child" could pick it up. She demanded that *Daddy's Roommate* and all other books with a gay "agenda" be moved to a special section of the library.

It was almost 90 degrees outside, and my town felt like it would explode. Karol's words tasted like acid in my mouth. Her letter was followed by a slew of media coverage and other letters to the editor. Patrons of the library, religious leaders, teachers, and members of gay and lesbian coalitions all over Vermont wrote letters. Everywhere I went people had something to say about the library and Karol Jones. Some national newspapers and local TV stations began to follow the debate.

Karol continued to write letters, each attacking homosexuality with greater fervor. She claimed homosexuals were sexual deviants, perverts, with a propensity to recruit children and commit sodomy. If exposed to homosexuality, children would invariably be corrupted.

This was my family she was talking about. I felt frozen and numb when I read her letters, like some wild creature caught in a bright light. I was the innocent child she was struggling to defend, and my mother the evil demon that she would have jailed or burned.

I bought a copy of *Daddy's Roommate* and my heart broke for that little boy fishing with his father's lover. What would it have meant for me to have had this book when I was 12? It may or may not have changed my struggles, but at least I might have identified with that boy and found some comfort in the understanding that someone shared my experience. What did she mean, "corrupted"? What did she mean, "recruit"? Nothing of what that woman said rang true for me, and yet she said it to identify my life and my family.

All of this was on my mind when the library announced they would hold a public hearing, so any member of the community could come and speak their piece about the issue.

I had so much to say, but to say it out loud would change my life completely. To say that my mother is a lesbian would be to face all the reasons I had remained silent for so long. But to *not* speak would be a disservice to my community and to the women who raised me.

I went to the meeting. The room was sweltering. There was scattered applause, ranting, hissing, screaming, laughing, affirmations, and jeering. When my name was called it took all of my energy to lift my body and walk to the microphone. But as I opened my mouth to speak I realized the weight of that moment—I was ending six years of frightened silence:

"My name is Erin Gluckman. I am 16 years old. I have been living with my lesbian mother and her partner for six years. Let me clear one thing up. I am straight. I like men. I am an example directly opposite to the panic that has been raised, and I am not the only one. I am speaking for the children of straight and lesbian parents when I say it is imperative that information regarding different lifestyles be freely available.

"I am angry that, because of one woman's ignorance, access to the book *Daddy's Roommate* could be limited for children in need of information. I am angry that normalcy is being defined in such limiting terms. I am angry that Karol is proposing the falsehood that homosexuals engage in recruiting children and the misconception that one's sexuality is a choice. In our home there are books about being gay and they have been available for me to read. I can say that none of them has ever influenced me to change my sexuality. As a minor who is dependent on the library for free access to information, I trust you to uphold the Library Bill of Rights."

* * *

The Library Board of Trustees chose to leave the book *Daddy's Roommate* in the children's section of the library. Hearing this news made me feel like I could breathe again. Knowing I was a part of this victory, knowing I had spoken out helped me to feel like I was finally real to the rest of the world. To speak our identities is to make them real. For the first time, I had said out loud who I was.

In the next few years, I found a lot of political strength in my identity as the straight daughter of a lesbian mother. I found that as a heterosexual woman, my voice was listened to, and in this way I could defend my mother, her lover, and our family. I also discovered I was bicultural. I sat on the borderlines of queer and straight. It took a while, but eventually I fell in love with this identity. I was culturally queer, sexually straight.

Today, I am 20 years old. Two years ago I left my small town in Vermont for college in western Massachusetts. Last winter I walked into the dining commons at my small liberal arts college, and sitting with all my friends was a woman with short hair, laughing eyes, a leather jacket, and a smile that made my stomach drop. I felt the weight of some unknown emotion, some strange desire bearing down on me, and I pursued it for all I was worth. One month later I found myself on my bed, tasting the sweetness of her lips and begging her not to pull away. A month after that I told someone for the first time that I was bisexual.

My coming-out story is complicated and started nearly ten years ago. In the past year I have had long talks with my mother, both of us confronting the homophobia in ourselves that rose to the surface when I came out. I sometimes wonder what Karol Jones would think of me now. Have I turned into the recruited child? Can I speak powerfully anymore on my mother's behalf without the privileges of heterosexuality to cushion me? At 20 I feel as if I all of a sudden must relearn who I am. I cannot continue to speak the truth if I do not know what that truth is.

I have found the queer community to be amazingly dynamic but terribly uncomfortable with its diversity. Here, of all places, I did not expect to be confronted with binary systems of identification, but it is here that I have struggled the most with this polar language: homosexual or heterosexual, gay or lesbian, male or female, butch or femme, top or bottom. I either find myself in none of these categories or all of them. Once again I ache to define myself not only in terms my community can understand but also that accurately describe who I am. I find myself roaming in the country of sexuality, wandering half out of choice and half in search of a language I can claim. Let me be a queer straight, the dyke who sleeps with men, the woman mistaken for a man. Let me have the best of these dichotomies. Let me speak with a language of my own.

When I was 16 and adamantly straight, I realized that I was a political creature by the nature of my mother's sexuality. Now, at 20, I am breaking the law every time I go to bed with another woman. Let this be who I am: an outlaw of desire, in the image of my mother, with a language all my own.

reate.

meicha, 23
Oklahoma and New Mexico

This process of coming to terms with my sexual identity has been a long haul. Growing up Southern Baptist in a small town in Oklahoma offered little preparation for a healthy sexuality of any type, especially a queer one. After recovering from sermons on lust and sin, I began to realize that I was who the preacher had been ranting about when he said, "God created Adam and Eve, not Adam and Steve."

I came out to my mom a few months ago, and when she regained consciousness she said two things: "Honey, you're going to get AIDS" (because we all know, the disease is God's punishment for the evil of same-sex eroticism) and then, "Bisexual? Michelle, you gotta make up your mind."

Mom, I have. I exist to challenge the status quo. I laugh and love—even those who don't love me—because love, after all, is the only reason good enough for revolution.

Our Story

I tried to write it, first as a story, then as a poem—what my friend Christine had told me, about the rape. I had just read Marge Piercy, who talks about being a voice for the voiceless, and I envisioned this story could do that, that I could somehow write about the injustice,

the way Christine was raped before he ever touched her, the way, once she knew she was being followed, she just walked into the woods and waited, resigned. And then the curtain, the so-many-years memory, the won't-leave-me-alone memory of the violence that day in the woods; until the day the curtain rips and she sees for the first time clearly: herself laying motionless against autumn leaves without a scratch. But the violence,

the violence was there, the seeds planted many years before, by drunken hands and broken lips; like the man who told her how lucky she was to be with him now that she was gaining weight because most men wouldn't put up with hips like that. Other stories too. So many other words, entering and entering between her thighs; the cock thrusting without her permission, without my permission, and all the lies we've lay under all this time just waiting, waiting,

waiting for it all to be over, so we can stand up and try to brush off the memory like the crusted leaves. And I say to myself, Christine, I am in your story. It is my story. And I cannot be a voice for the voiceless, I cannot speak *to* the oppressed

but *of* them, as they are in me. They are me. The only reason, the only reason I write any of this is because I have to tell some-one. It is my story. It is our story.

Ariana Banias, 19
Wilmette, Ill.

I am a Greek-American student at Sarah Lawrence College studying poetry, sociology, and literature. I am interested in writing that deals with gender identity, sexuality, class, race, and ethnicity, and will be working on an undergraduate senior thesis on poetry and politics during my senior year. The poem "Chicago Heights, 1984" speaks not only about how I saw my male cousin as proud and tough but also about my envy of his strength as part of a masculine identity I wasn't allowed to participate in or express.

Chicago Heights, 1984

The summer we lived at my cousin's house with a lean,
        reaching tree in front,
we picked its berries, green pebbles we whipped at each other
        like young bullets,
our pockets bulging with their hidden bulk. This was how we
        competed, pulling off
thin stems that joined the round fruits; each one, a singular
        missile, compact and burning
for the throw. At 8 years old, he couldn't dream up a dare
I wouldn't do, and I envied his easy pride—how he took the
        flame of each tiny, stinging impact
like ordinary fire, a stone, never showing that its heat even
        entered him.

Shane Luitjens, aka Torque, 23
Bloomington-Normal, Ill.

Originally from Bloomington-Normal, Ill., I am a graduate of Drake University living in the Seattle area, where I work as a graphic designer. I spend my free time teaching and programming youth arts events. I enjoy writing, reading, hiking, rowing, music, and challenges. I am a queer theorist and a spoken word artist. I enjoy it because spoken word and slam poetry has no boundaries. It is the way we speak. It is the way we think. It is a movement to take poetry back into the mouth, the place it came from. We are all hungry, and I envision spoken word as the only way to reach the insides of the body. I am the author of *Every Ineloquency* (Torque Creations, 1997) and *Blood for Wings, Part One* (Torque Creations, 1998).

I Wish I Knew the Last Four Verses of America the Beautiful

I need a dollar,
dollar and a half.
Maybe just a couple quarters
and some pennies.
I need some money to buy bombs
and save America.
She's sinking fast.
We're high noon
down at the OK,
corralled
into the great white fight
for freedom
or at least a buy-one-get-one freedom.

        And the price is right
to be a man in an Armani or Versace
        suit
asking me if I'd like another drink
with my phone number,
but
I don't even know you
or the field your cotton came from,
not dumb,
but wondering
if you think I am another piece of the rock,
        Plymouth,
        my mouth just looking to be stabbed by a fag with
        a flag

who tells me I would look better in
his plot of land.
So take a ride,
a drive,

off the corners as you get off the 99
to Western and Wall,
where the black and Latino men stack up on the side of the
road
balled up in little unemployed bunches like words in a sentence
that runs on
in poems on bottoms of paper cups
piled mile high
from the AA meetings
that are this nation of ours.

My name is Shane and I am an American—
I have been one for 22 years and counting—
don't plan on stopping anytime soon
'cause I've got a war to win
for the A-M-E-R-I
C to shining C a future
for us here, Mr.
The two of us
quilting flags
in the 'burbs
we fought
so hard
for so
long?

I know America

I love America,
and I'd sing her stone dress, torchlight tiara
if I could get past the first verse
about liberty
while you look at my ass
and I must want you to look
like the men at Elliot and Wall
want to be seen
'cause I need a job
to make some money
to make America
in fast food flophouses,
outlet stores,
and men in Armani and Versace
got me
dreaming
in a dress
high heels
mascara
call me Liberty, and

I could be President
with my inability to accessorize
but I can fix that—
just a dollar
and a little change
just a little change can't hurt—
turning our hard-earned money
built by the backs of those
we couldn't even name if we tried
to build a bomb to obliterate
the weak and the hungry, the tired and the cold

and the French
'cause they have always
had smarter choices
when it comes to evening wear.

So no, I don't need another drink,
I'll just take the dollar.
Maybe a dollar and a half.
And a piece of the rock.

reate,

Gloria Ng, 19
San Francisco, Calif.

I am a 19-year-old Chinese-American, born in Hong Kong and raised in San Francisco. I came to the United States when I was 1 year old. I grew up with my parents, who spent most of their time out of the house working to survive. Indoctrinated with the Bill of Rights in grade school, I am quick to see hypocrisy and bigotry, and I am attempting to translate silenced anger into words.

gloria ng

Letter from a Young Queer Working-Class Woman of Color

As I complete my junior year of college I am finally able to make clear and confident decisions about my direction in life. In high school it was so easy to follow one fork and listen to someone else—to my father, who provided the financial assistance, to my Eurocentric teachers, who defined what was legitimate knowledge, to my peers, who would only accept me for someone I was not. Now I see many possibilities; the difficult part is finding out where I want to go.

Whatever age you may be, I ask you to educe the you that knows you best. This act of self-reflection will help you become the best possible you. Be honest with yourself. Even though it may be hard to admit you are hurt and angry, living through it and feeling it will make you stronger. Try not to block out your feelings; they tell you something. Building a wall only makes it harder to see beyond it and to connect with people who really care. When you hear yourself, listen.

Looking back at my high school years, I realize all I wanted was someone to tell me that it was OK to be me. All I wanted was someone to affirm where I came from and where I was headed. To tell me it was OK to be:

1. a woman
2. Chinese-American (or, to be more general, "of color")
3. young
4. queer
5. sexual with oneself
6. "fat"
7. poor
8. single

Instead, when I was younger, women were not encouraged to speak. Whenever I spoke my mind I was scolded by my parents and teachers for "talking back" or told by my friends that I was "not cool." They all reminded me to "be nice" and "know my place." Essentially, they were saying I should deny my own feelings. I found myself asking: Why can't I fit in? What is wrong with me? Is there something I'm not getting? Maybe they were right. Maybe I was dumb.

In elementary school many of my Asian-American peers sang on the playground. *Ching, chong, Chinaman, sitting on a wall...* My Asian-American male peers sang to taunt other Asian-American male peers to do something "manly." Otherwise, they would accuse them of being chicken and tell them to "go back to China," even when they were born in America. I was called a "chink" too, and I could not understand why my Asian-American peers spouted that derogatory term.

In every grade, people different from their peers were labeled "weird." Accusations of people being "gay," if they were male, or "fruity," if they were female, would most often follow. If others thought something I said was "weird," I would quickly say I was "just joking" and laugh it off even though I was the only one laughing. I'd turn red under people's gazes and look away. I was learning shame, learning guilt.

Whenever I would ask my parents "Why?," they'd say I was too young to understand. They'd never take me seriously. They'd say that I'd understand when I got older. I understood a lot more than they gave me credit for.

As early as elementary school I had feelings for both males and females. Somehow or another I knew my feelings for females were rejected. I tried to block out the feelings I had for females and focus on the ones I had for males. I never really had a best friend. I kept a lot of thoughts and feelings to myself. I wanted to be accepted even if it meant being accepted for what others wanted me to be, not who I was.

I discovered masturbation when I was nine. But because of other Christian peers and teachers, I learned it was not OK. According to them, the only time a woman should be sexual was after she got married. My parents did not talk about sex or sexual orientation. The only thing my mother told me was, "Don't get raped." She did not describe what it meant to be raped, let alone what it meant to have a healthy relationship, to have sexual intercourse, or the consequences thereof. How was I to know how I could protect myself? How could I protect myself when I wasn't confident in my own body?

For an Asian-American female, I was considered "larger" than most of my peers. I was constantly picked on for my weight, my hairstyle, my wardrobe, the size of my wardrobe, the thickness of my eyebrows, my hairy arms and neck, my handwriting, my drawings, my abilities. I tried dieting in third grade and got in trouble when my mom found out I was not eating lunch. I tried eating less, starving. I exercised for hours a day when I could and especially at night when my parents thought I was asleep. I would move in silence, for fear of waking anyone. I weighed myself constantly, sometimes five times a day. Some days I would not want to go to school because I was embarrassed I had gained one pound and felt fat.

After years, I am still learning to love my body. I am still unlearning self-hatred and self-doubt. I can tell you more about various circumstances in which I have felt hurt, but I think I have provided you enough examples for you to understand the cycles of self-sabotage. In a time when institutions such as the media, family, and school tell you who you are or who you are supposed to be, it's easy to be insecure about yourself, to doubt yourself, to hate who you are and begin believing what they say. Sometimes it is even easier to start behaving the way they want you to behave.

But it is so important to learn to be true to yourself—find your own passions and talents. Growing up working class, I could not afford expensive hobbies such as photography, art, sculpture, travel, etc. Instead, I started writing and continue to this day. I write now to remind you to look inside yourself for the answers, to always be conscious of what you are buying into. Whose standards are you living by? What stereotypes have you learned? Unlearn the messages that help destroy you. Decolonize your mind. Create your own messages. Listen to your own voice. Live by it. Die by it.

It is OK for you to be single. Hey, I am 19. I am bisexual. I still have not been in any relationship more serious than friendship yet. Get involved when you are ready. People can label you a "late bloomer" as much as they want. They have reasons to belittle you; most often, they want to make themselves feel better. Be true to yourself. Follow your own timeline.

In no particular order unless specified, it is important that you:

1. Understand and know yourself first.

2. Accept and love yourself.

3. Keep in touch with your feelings. They are as important as anyone else's.

4. Listen to yourself. Listen to your body. If you are hurting, if you are tired, your body is telling you something.

5. Choose. You have options. People may want to hide them from you. Find them. You can decide where you want to go, what you want to do, with what you learn.

6. Resist. People can make things hard for you, but you can fight; you have a voice. You are not alone—you have many voices within you; find them.

7. Find support. Find people who have your best interest at

heart. Do not assume you will automatically connect with another person just because that person shares the same race, class, gender, sexual orientation, or religion.

8. Share. Sharing space is different from taking space. We can understand a lot from our differences, why some are privileged, why some are persecuted.

9. Always keep an open mind. Listen to what others have to tell you. Respect them. You may agree or disagree with them. Maintain dialogue. Take what you need.

10. Give back. Empower others. Mentor. Liberate.

11. Remember the pain as well as the happiness. It makes you human. You can keep learning and understanding and relating to so much more when you remember.

12. Build on those who came before you, build with those who are with you, make sure others who follow can continue building after you.

13. ______________________. Fill in the blank(s). This is just a partial list.

Knowledge is easy to gain. "Claim your education." —Adrienne Rich

Yours for a Revolutionary Democracy,
Someone Who Loves You

Thea Gahr, 19
McMinnville, Ore.

I grew up on a farm in the outskirts of a small town in Oregon. I lived way far out in the boonies, some would say, I would say. The closest neighbor lived just under a mile away.

I grew up in a family large enough to be its own village. I'm the youngest. My house was the miniature version of a cultural melting pot. Today, only traces exist of the lives that have been through these doors. The stories are saved up for long, dark, restless nights.

I can't review what it was like, my life; it comes in fragments. It's not the details that have made me who I am, nor do they explain why I think what I think. A million people in through unlocked doors. Doors that extended to fields and mountains. Car doors that opened and took me along. To go...to go... I love to go and be here or there. So I won't try to explain. But I want you to know I'm grateful to be alive.

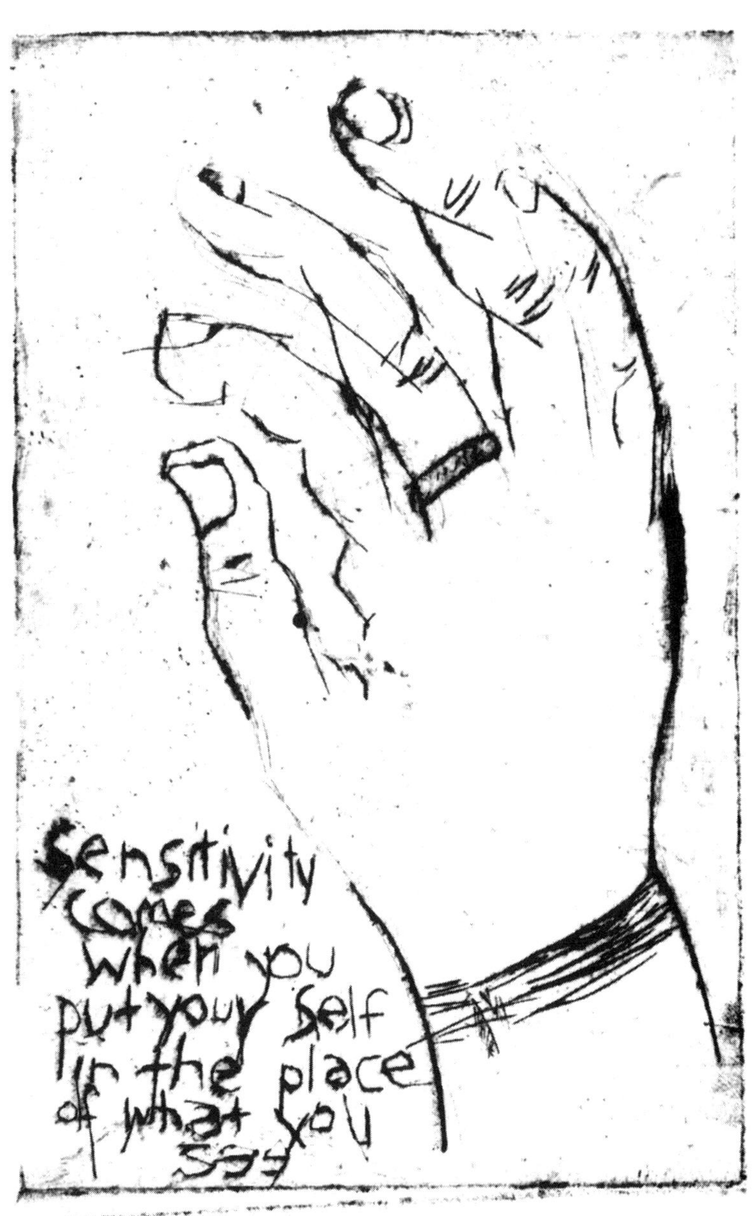

Sensitivity comes..., dry point etching, 3.5" x 5.5", 1997

Untitled, dry point etching, 3.5” x 5.5”, 1997

reate.

John Frazier, 24
Ridgeland, S.C.

I am a poet and recently completed a book of poems on love and geography called *Real Sugar*. The poems were influenced by a recent trip to North Africa and France. My work explores themes of race, sexuality, class, and intersections of these identities.

john frazier

Another Country

We have come here
in our meaning to each other
still searching behind the proud space

for forgiveness.
Behind the space: a wasted heaven or
your village in ruins. And this is chasm,

stiffly measured.
How much do you love me?
Bigger than these arms,

outstretched, creating a galaxy of silent
asking: Is it not about soft suicides
but knowing edges?

Hand me a penny,
so I can make a too big wish,
so I can pretend to forgive you

for giving me up.

T. Rowan, 16
New York

I began my coming-out process at 13, and my writing and art have helped me through it all. I am 16, Jewish, and queer. Activism, writing, improvisation, hiking, reading, messing with people's assumptions about gender, and questioning the status quo are all passions of mine. It took me a while to learn to find power in words that have been used to hurt me, such as *dyke, butch*, and *queer*, but now I have reclaimed them for myself.

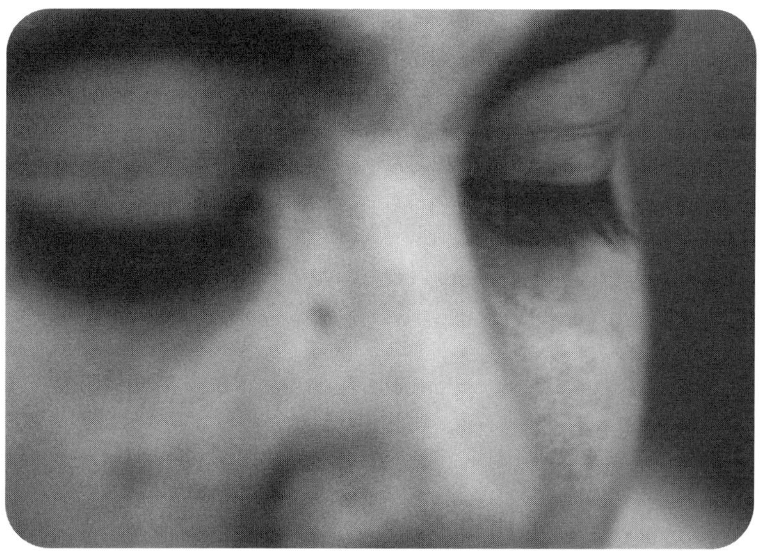

Walking Home

It is nighttime, and the Old Boulevard church bells will soon chime midnight, but we are too far uptown to hear them. Rebecca and I are walking in silence, shoulder to shoulder, down the uneven sidewalk, heading home after a late movie. We are trying to make the best of every second of the last few weeks of summer, enjoying being in each other's presence, savoring the communicative silence we are sharing. I want to take her hand in mine, but it is dark, and the absence of passersby on either side of the street makes me more cautious, not less. It's not worth the risk. I walk faster, with a determination that does not reflect how I feel inside. I tell Rebecca about an article I read in a magazine that said your posture and stride can increase or decrease your chances of being attacked. Men aren't as likely to prey on determined-looking women walking purposefully, their heads raised and feet firm. Knowing I've always had a strong stride (even when I wished I was more graceful) helps me brave the rest of the walk home.

We approach an intersection. Rebecca points out how quiet and empty the streets are. I love the silence and the puddles of light the streetlamps cast on the sidewalk in the sticky August heat. When we are a few feet from the crosswalk, we see a nondescript car approach. It slows down near us, and some men stick their heads out of the windows.

"Fucking dykes!" they yell, followed by more slurs and swears. They turn the corner and speed off onto a side street. I stand still for a moment, then we continue on our way. I hold my head up, pretending I didn't notice what just happened. Rebecca laughs and wonders out loud whether they thought we were a couple, and if so, why? After all, we are only friends, not lovers, she reminds me, and she is straight as a board. She says jokingly yet truthfully, "Sorry, man, I'm not a dyke, but both my best friends are." I laugh halfheartedly. She wonders if we emit visual signals that we are lesbians and what they might be. I can't relate to her sincere but humorous analysis. My stomach is in my throat. What if they come after us? What if next time they decide to chase us instead of swerving onto a side street? To her, having "dyke" yelled out of a car window is humorous. "They're so stupid, they can't think of anything better to say," says Rebecca. To me, it is an attack on my existence. I know these were boys from my school who know I am a lesbian. Maybe they saw my girlfriend and me holding hands in the hallway near the gymnasium when we thought no one was looking, maybe they've just heard rumors. Either way, they know. This is no random assault.

* * *

I use the word *dyke* with my friends who are gay, lesbian, and bisexual in a friendly, affirming way. I even find tremendous strength in it. But when it is hurled as a slur, I fear. I can tell Rebecca is more upset by this incident than she lets on. I don't mention anything about it and suggest we stop at the convenience store for ice cream. I don't want her to know that a few words slung maliciously by a bunch of hormone-filled high school students fill me with fear and anger. *Why do my friends always have to be involved?* I ask myself. I would rather deal with this alone. This is about me, not Rebecca. I want to protect her from understanding what I have to deal with every time I walk down the halls at school or home from the movie theater. She doesn't need to deal with this, doesn't need to be the victim of an attack on me. Above all, I don't want her to know I am weaker than I seem. She knows many of my insecurities, my vulnerabilities. But I still have to let on that I am strong, show her I am as strong and confident as ever.

* * *

I listen to the sound of our sandals pounding the sidewalk. I make small talk about the movie we just saw, predictions about what next semester might hold for us, comments on the cool breeze that is relieving some of the unrelenting heat. But behind my facade of nonchalance, which I won't let my closest friend and soul sister see through, I am shaking. Behind this mask of composure and calmness, I am a shaking like a scared little girl.

Labels, Names, & Identity

My sexuality is as fluid, infinite, undefinable, and ever-changing as the north-flowing river that runs through the valley where I have spent nearly all my life. The continuum of sexuality is long, and I am always slip-sliding from one side to the other and most often stopping to rest somewhere in the middle. Sexuality is not black or white...it is gray, and gray comes in infinite shades, more than could ever be contained in the biggest box of drawing pencils.

I know who I am. Being unable to fit into a narrow category defined by someone else is not confusion. I know that defining myself is not so simple. If I collect all the labels that apply to me—Jewish-pagan-vegan-bisexual-lesbian-queer-woman-girl-womyn-grrrl—I would quickly fill up a book. Everyone's sexuality is unique, just as no two maple leaves on the trees surrounding my parents' house are the same as they transform into fiery red, orange, and yellow each autumn. That is part of what makes us human. The unnatural society we have imposed on the natural world is based on polarity and dichotomy. But we are constantly transforming, developing, and changing. Nothing is as simple as yes or no, right or wrong.

My sexuality is part of my Self, and my Self cannot be explained in words. I do not have to answer to anyone. I do not need to decide on a term for myself just to make myself easier for someone else to understand. I owe no explanation. Either/or does not work for me. I am changing every day and hope this transformation is endless. My identity is more vast than can be encompassed by one word. My love is beyond definition and needs no justification.

reate.

Siobhan Brooks, 25
San Francisco, Calif.

I work at the Lusty Lady theater in San Francisco, and I am a union organizer. The following interview is excerpted from my book in progress called *Dancing in the Shadows: Interviews with Men and Women Sex Workers of Color*. I think this interview will help further educate people about some of the working conditions and issues in the sex industry.

Dancing in the Shadows, an interview

Minal is a young queer from India and has been a sex worker in the S/M scene for a year and a half. He has taken a break from sex work and lives in San Francisco. In this interview Minal talks about his journey into sex work as a way of uplifting his self-esteem around body-image issues, his feeling of empowerment doing sex work in drag, his experience coming to the United States from India, and being queer while coming to terms with identifying as being transgender.

Siobhan Brooks: How did your parents accept the fact that you're gay?

Minal: I told them I was gay and giving up religion at the same time, but they were most upset that I was giving up religion. They thought that without religion I would be lost and never come back to the "path of righteousness." But they were alright. I was living at home then, and they were accepting. The drag upset them a lot, more than the gay stuff. They were hoping that I would have an arranged marriage, and I told them if they could find me a husband, I'd be willing to settle down. [*Laughs*]

S: Are you in school?

M: I just finished law school and took the bar, and when I find out my results I'll look for a nonprofit job. I know I don't want to be a lawyer.

S: How did you get into sex work?

M: Well, before I get into that I have to tell you how I got into S/M generally, since I used to be a complete vanilla bottom. I'm gay, by the way; I'm exploring being transgendered, and I've been doing drag for about ten years, on and off. Drag was never a sexual thing for me, I've always had sex "as a guy." Around March of last year a friend asked me about rape fantasies—she wanted to know what my fantasies were. I realized I hadn't been fantasizing at all. When I did start thinking about it, my fantasies were all about whipping. I started reading up on S/M, and it was making me interested in sex for the first time. Before, I never knew what the big deal was with sex. I put a personal ad in the paper to do scenes with different people, and I realized that for what I was doing, I could be getting good money. I had a lot of friends in the sex industry who were asking me, "Why aren't you charging for what you're doing?"

So that summer I did it for free and learned what I needed to do, and by November I started putting out ads in the *Bay Area Reporter*. My ads were sort of genderfuck: my picture was taken from the neck down in a corset, fishnets and garter belt. It was a dom-type look. I realized there weren't that many guys into doing S/M professionally, and the ones that were were really butch—so I stood out a lot. It was great. It was the first time I had really good sex, I was getting paid for it, and I felt totally in control. It was good, but I was wondering how many people I was losing by advertising as a fem dom. I started putting ads online without the fem look and got a lot more response, so I switched to just having a nude picture in the paper as opposed to a girlish one. The responses were more than I could handle, which is a good thing. That's how I got into sex work, as a way of exploring my sexuality.

S: Are you concerned about how doing sex work affects your intimate relationships?

M: Yes, I'm concerned. The scenes that I do for free just feel so different that I start wondering what does it mean to do this over an extended period of time, where you just feel so disconnected. It can become routine. When I first started doing sex work it was a little difficult, but now it's no big deal to do a scene—what does that mean when sex loses all its specialness? I'm lucky, because with S/M I'm totally engaged in a scene, the power exchange is always real. But it has to take its toll on me in some way in terms of my ability to be intimate.

S: Can you talk a bit about being transgender?

M: My tranny side...I'm not sure what all it means to me right now. My best friend was a really butch dyke, and she and I were dealing with transgendered issues together, like reading up on the theory and the laws. Anyway, he transitioned a couple of weeks ago...and it was weird, even after reading transgendered theory, to have my best friend transition and become FTM. It pushed a lot of my buttons. It made me think about where I was going with my transgenderism, or what does it mean. For me, drag was never about being a "drag queen." I felt I had to do it. I felt I had to express the woman inside of me, and when I did it, it always felt very real. But does that mean that I'm going to transition, or does it mean that I'm just a cross-dresser, or something else? I don't know. I use the term *transgender* as an umbrella that includes transsexuals and cross-dressers—pretty much anyone who is gender deviant in a way that is more than just genderfuck. I don't really know what it means for me, and I hope I figure it out! [*Laughs*].

S: Your weight also played a big role in your self-image, but what else affected your ability to feel secure with yourself?

M: My color. When I first came out I lived in D.C. for a year, and it was very segregated. There's white bars and Black bars, no Brown bars. There were no Brown people at all. Well, a few Asians and few Latinos. It was just weird being a Brown person there. Then I lived in the Castro in San Francisco, and it was very upscale and white. After a year I had to get out. I moved to the lower Haight, which felt a lot better. I lived across the street from the projects, and there were people of color on the street all the time. But going back to my first year in the Castro and going to the sex clubs, I was one of few people of color—maybe one other Brown person, Black person, Asian person—very few East Asian people. It was only after I started shaping up that I would get any attention there, whereas there were white boys who were really out of shape and got attention. If you're a person of color, you have to overcompensate to get attention. When I left the vanilla places in the Castro I started going to S/M parties. There's a difference between the gay male S/M versus the more multigendered fetish ball scenes where every race and gender is represented. At the gay [white] male S/M clubs I never found anyone to play with. They were these big bear types, and the fact that I was a person of color and a fem top didn't go over very well. So my dungeon was my little place where I could create a space I felt comfortable in.

Usually, when people use the word *exotic* to describe me, that's one of the most racist things you can do. But in the sex-work context, it's different for me. A guy I negotiated online with (we had E-mailed each other back and forth) had responded to a picture I sent him of myself. His response was: "Your young, lithe, exotic beauty would be a joy to experience." [*Laughs*] Normally, I would be like, "There's no way I'm doing anything with you." But, again, it was for money, and he was paying $600 for this huge scene. In the scene I didn't feel exoticized, but obviously that was going on in his head. I'm willing to play the little "jungle boy" type thing, if that's what brings them in. At times I have mixed feelings about that, and I wonder how is prostituting my color different from selling my body. If they're willing to pay to exoticize me, that's different than just somebody exoticizing me. I don't know if that's a valid distinction, but frankly, I don't care if the distinction is valid or not. For me, that's the distinction that's working.

S: I think that's quite valid. For most women of color in the sex industry, it's mostly for the money. Sexuality and getting in touch with your eroticism comes later. Do you usually feel safe doing S/M scenes?

M: Pretty much. I try to avoid people who use speed. I remember this one guy came over and said he would like to do a scene but had just done a line of speed. He was a huge man, dressed all in black and wearing a ski mask with just his eyes showing. I let him in, and he turned out to be the sweetest thing, but it could have also been the last thing I ever did. [*Laughs*] Other times I just started feeling unsafe because the man was really big and acting strange, and I really didn't know how to defend myself. It was weird...in scenes like that I get nervous because most of the guys are bigger than me, and my whole dungeon is set up to restrain people. He could have just gagged me and tortured me to death; that's just too dangerous.

S: Again, in terms of gender, it's interesting to hear you talk about feeling unsafe because these are issues that—stereotypically—women usually worry about in sex work and life in general. How has your self-image improved from doing sex work?

M: I feel a lot more confident and secure with myself. I think that has a lot to do with S/M and coming into my own power.

reate.

Attar, 23
New Jersey

i go by the name of Attar because she was an ancient goddess of the land that is now known as lebanon, and for me she represents strength and wisdom. i am lebanese and come from a very diverse place in new jersey and so my writing is a reflection of that. i am 23 years old and active not only in the arab community but also in ethnic/feminist/queer communities. i have been writing since i was young; my journals were the only spaces i felt comfortable to be who i was, whatever that meant at the time. i know that, for me, writing helps me understand the complexities of my emotions and allows me the freedom to continue to challenge, grow, and change to become the person i need to be.

fingers
by Attar

visions of brown, slender fingers
grind through the deep hurt
painful   liberating
kneading away the sorrow
and erupting in me a happiness
i have only known for a year and a half
remembering   bitten-off nails
and sturdy fists
gentle but strong
masculine but woman enough

thinking about   aged olive hands
detailed with wrinkles of experience
and stories of passionate moments
and good times   but hard times
force felt through my woman-ness
such sweet love

searching still for those hands that will grip me,
hold me long enough to love me.

Antigona, 21
San Juan, Puerto Rico

I am a 21-year-old Puerto Rican lesbian. I am a profound paradox of cultural essence. I am a challenge.... I wrote this poem to help myself heal almost one year after coming out to my mother and undergoing an exorcism during Sunday Mass at her church. I am a survivor.

Straight-Out Pain

As they lay hands on me
I resist the cry...
I resist the pain of
Blazing hands that impose on me
The label of "evil."

I am OK! I can stand this!
I tell myself as the eyes of the congregation
glare at me.
I look at your eyes, Mother:
Is your love big enough?
Big enough to stop this?

I am OK! I can stand this!
This deliverance of Christian insanity cutting

Through my skin, blowing out my tears,
Poking my reality...
I hear the loud fanaticism:
I call the evils of lesbianism out! I free you from evil!
The ignorant slurs take possession of the silence,
Of my silence...

I cannot speak.
I cannot move.
They hold me down.
They shake me out.
Don't you understand nothing is coming out from me!!!
Are you really expecting a miracle?

I am OK! I can stand this!
This oppressing fear of entangled faith
The hands are burning me....
The hands are burning....

Burning me down to an emotional battlefield.

I struggle.
I struggle.
I reach for you, Mother
As you stand there
Embracing ignorance.
As you comply.
Is your love big enough?
Big enough to stop this?

Straight-out pain has embraced me.
Let me go now.
I say: Let me go now!
Let me go and free me
From your game of advertising miracles.

reate.

Cecilia Isaacs-Blundin, 17
Wallingford, Penn.

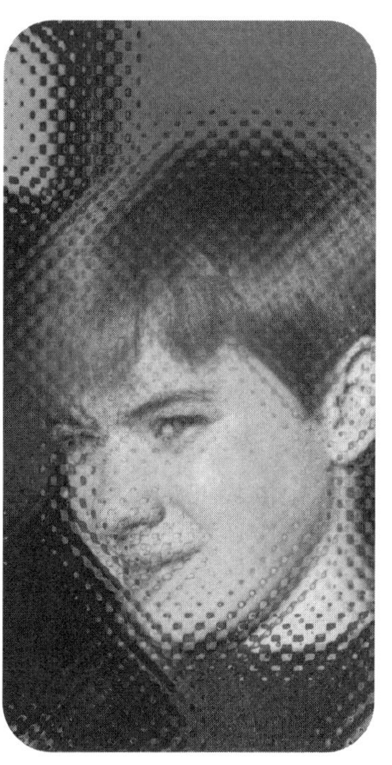

I was born to two former hippie types who teach kindergarten in Philadelphia. I attribute much of my creative talent to their good humor. I am a senior at Strath Haven High School in Wallingford, Penn. I do a lot of distance running, trumpet playing in a ska band, and community service (e.g., Youth Aid Panel, Red Cross, feeding the homeless, and a bunch of other stuff, but this is starting to sound like a college application). Yeah, I identify as a lesbian, and in fact, I was the first out kid at my school. My girlfriend, Arden, and I were the first gay couple to attend a dance together (her senior ball). This year I have begun a straight/bi/gay alliance at school.

cecilia isaacs-blundin

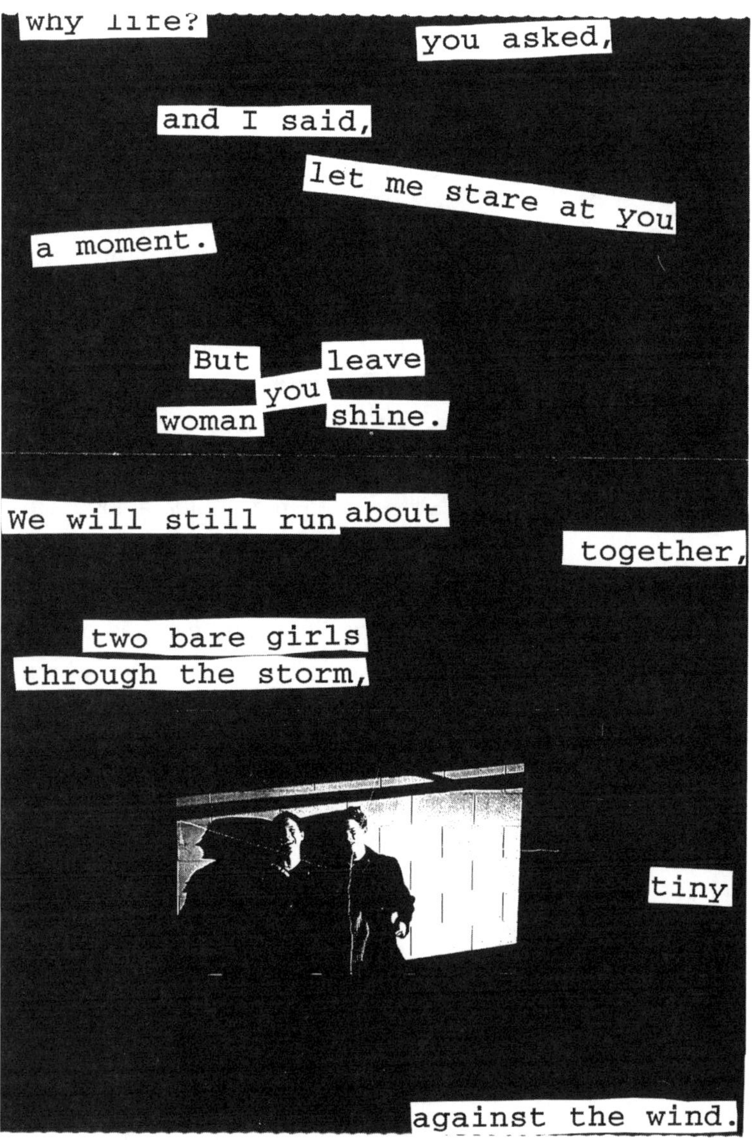
why life?
you asked,
and I said,
let me stare at you
a moment.
But
leave
you
woman
shine.
We will still run about
together,
two bare girls
through the storm,
tiny
against the wind.

why life?, mixed media collage, 11" x 17", 1997

Emil Keliane, 25
Shiraz, Iran/Chicago, Ill.

I was born August 12, 1973 in Shiraz, Iran. I have lived in Tabriz, Iran; Tehran, Iran; Chicago, Ill; Rogersville, Tenn.; Fremont, Calif.; San Jose, Calif.; and Santa Rosa, Calif., and now live in Marin County, Calif, where I hope to remain for a long time. English is my third language but has become my challenge, passion, friend, and artistic voice. I began keeping a diary at the age of 16, and over the past ten years the diary has become my writing gymnasium where I attempt poetic exercises and artistic leaps. I graduated from St. Gregory High School in Chicago as student of the year, and have been going to college on and off since then. These entries were written between 1995–1998. This is my first published work.

Diary Excerpts, 1995-1998

When earthbound and gagged, when obligated to trivial daily tasks, I begin to dream, and fiercely. I step out of my station, role, and mood to seek the sky because it is arbitrary, universal, and temperamental, like a poet; emotional and expansive, like a poet. The clouds like words he would use to express his many moods: now light, now dark, now still, now nomadic—traveling madly.

Maybe this is why Mother and I spend so much time in the yard these days: Once we were forced to flee our country, our home, and this escape became a pattern, and this pattern became a restlessness that drove us out into the yard, under the stars, because the sky was the only familiar thing between here and Iran.

Mother and I are in the yard again. She's chewing sunflower seeds and doing a crossword puzzle. She is sentimental about this particular puzzle book because it comes from Iran; the clues are printed in Farsy. She even paused once, placed the open page to her face and breathed in the yellowed paper, speaking wistfully. I'm relieved to see her display such soft, childlike sentimentality. I was beginning to feel totally unrelated to her, as she has a tendency to be withdrawn, despondent.

* * *

In Tabriz when I was about 5 years old, I remember Mother and Father examining a peculiar paper that was hard and unbending, with black and white shapes that were indecipherable but fascinating. I asked them what this strange new thing was in our home and wondered silently how my own parents could be so totally enthralled by it. Dad said it was a picture of Mom—the simplest way he saw fit to describe an X-ray to a 5-year-old.

A picture of Mom! I saw no resemblance no matter how hard I looked. Squinting helped none. It was evident that the world of adults was to remain a mystery to us children. They even saw things differently.

Little did I know then that our disparate views, my parents' and my own, would rarely find unity; that even in adulthood they would always see me from a distorted perspective, a mangled portrait not too dissimilar from an X-ray; that one day I would go to them in need and offer them the gift of five beautiful and provocative words: I think I am gay. A gift they would never unwrap, and a thing they would keep locked in a box and hidden away for always....

* * *

Some days I awake to regrets like that of a wild animal that has allowed itself to be brutally domesticated. These are moments when I am not in accord with the American culture, when I feel the puerility of having to keep up with trends, when I misplace my essential self, when I am ordering food from a much-too-sumptuous menu, when I am lost in the labyrinthine aisles of a supermarket, when I say a thing I don't mean, when I miss wholeheartedly and can smell the fecund soil of the village where my father was born.

* * *

I grew up always in battle. Aside from the Iran–Iraq war, there existed my parents' loveless marriage: a union of differing goals, needs, and wishes. Nineteen years of this. Although most marriages in Iran were generally undemonstrative, especially during the war when the entire populace seemed to slip into a mandatory state of grief and sobriety, I still sensed the absence of kisses, of tenderness, of playfulness. Somehow, naturally, I knew these were missing. Besides, romance was laughed at and considered a silly frivolity for the Westerner.

Over the course of my parents' marriage the rift grew larger and larger, wider and deeper. And I learned belligerence. I used the same tactics I witnessed my parents use against each other when I was old enough to recognize my own anger for them—when I was old enough to resent them for the wars, the battles. I grew angrier, Mom grew more and more despondent until she was flat-out depressed, and Dad graduated from social drinker to solitary alcoholic.

So I know about anger, about quarrels. I know them well. I know them intimately, and I don't want this knowledge to navigate my life. I don't want the anger to influence me in writing. I am first and foremost tender, then I am violent. And as a creative person, I fear anger most because it is unresolved anger that turns poet into politician.

* * *

It's ironic that in an attempt to become personally integrated in a world averse to homosexuality there would have to take place within me a heterosexual marriage of my male and female counterparts.

All my life I have tried to fathom my own gender fate. In relation to other men, am I man or am I woman? As a developing homosexual child in Iran, I learned to adopt women's sentiments concerning men and relationships—not a liberated, enlightened, independent woman's sentiments, but a subjugated woman's. I learned to feel and be inferior to man.

Like the subjugated woman, the universal homosexual must fight for his own liberation, because man will not hand it to him freely.

Still, I cannot repudiate the man in myself simply because he may possess tyrannical tendencies. Equally functioning within me are the two genders. I make decisions not as strictly woman, or solely man, but as an androgynous spirit. In taste, in temperament, in identifying with and relating to others, and in general perception of the world, I am two sexes. This is true not because I am gay but because I am human and arrive from woman's womb as well as man's. I come from the intuitive and psychic womb of my father's and my mother's physiological imagination. And I refuse to betray either force existing within me.

I solely repudiate the homophobe in me, the misogynist in me, the racist in me, the bigot in me.

And I will remain preoccupied with this bridging of a Siamese bond the world broke because it was viewed as unhealthy and freakish until I have arrived at a total state of integration on a personal and spiritual level.

Man placed a veil on woman's face to cloak his own knowledge and the truth that he would indubitably be extinct without her.

* * *

After 14 years of living in America I realize I am neither entirely Assyrian nor entirely American. I am like the migrant bird that vacillates from one sentiment to the other despite a season's demand, collecting along the route songs of all nations. (After all, it is not the color of one's skin that draws me to a person but the hues, the shades, the intensity of one's compassion!)

Tonight I feel, again, that shifting of cultural identities within me. The Assyrian and the American meet, and the space between them shifts as the forming continents did millions of years ago. Earthquakes! Spiritual tremors.

I will not choose one culture over the other. I will not limit myself to one devotion that might imprison me to many prejudices. I want to be—like the sky and the poet—universal, all-encompassing, and sympathetic to all possibilities. I choose the culture of universal and emotional acclimation. America issues me a card, a semi-identity that reads "Resident Alien," but I know I am a citizen…of hope, of borderless dreams, and of expansive living, loving.

reate.

Margot Kelley Rodriguez, 19
San Diego, Calif.

I grew up in San Diego and came out at 14. My mom says writing comes naturally to me because I was always making up stories when I was little. I write for survival. I write as a young queer Chicana in a society determined to silence me. I write to cross borders. Writing for me is intrinsically tied to justice and truth. I use writing and speaking as tools to organize for change. As a youth activist and writer I helped to form a queer and questioning youth writing and performance group called Queer Players. I received a community service award from San Diego Pride in 1996. I am a graduate of the first NGLTF Youth Leadership Institute and had the honor of keynoting the first ever Queer Latina/o Youth Conference at UCLA. I now work under professor and poet June Jordan with her program Poetry for the People at UC Berkeley, where I am completing my junior year as an ethnic studies major.

margot kelley rodriguez

Blessed are those who are persecuted for righteousness's sake. —Matthew 5:10

Heaven and Earth shall pass away, but my words will not pass away. —Matthew 24:35

Poem For Matthew Shepard

and I wonder
if at 32 degrees
the frost covered your hair
like a halo hiding
the crushed edges of your skull

And I wonder
if the sun cringed
if the morning cried
for your body strung along the fence
a boy beaten
a boy broken
I wonder if blood
cried out from the cuts
lining your torso
I wonder
if you heard the familiar
scraping of knife to scalp
the crack of a white fist
pounding brown bodies

And I wonder when we will stop
crucifying our children
along lonely stretches of Wyoming road

in Las Vegas bathroom stalls
behind pickup trucks in Texas
And I wonder
how many more Jameses
how many more Sherrices
how many more Matthews
will it take
for us
to say together
no more.

Manifesto

the sun creeps across my pillow
and I burrow my face into your neck
you smelling of sweet sleep and jasmine
and I think maybe
one morning soon
me and you could just lie here drinking in
the morning breeze as it tickles
the wind chimes
the curtains kissing us
awake
and maybe I could just lie here
holding you close maybe
one morning
I won't have to fly
out of this room
ten minutes behind
with no time to whisper
te quiero

in your ear
and maybe one morning
the paper won't greet me
with the haunted faces of refugees
the latest bombing assault
murder of our peoples
maybe the front page will display
Marcos unmasked and triumphant
Mumia will walk down Philly streets
so I won't wake up
so tense
or have to rush up
Telegraph bent over
the weight of books on my back
shins splinting
and sweat gathering at the base of my neck
and maybe
someday
I won't have to crawl through classes
that never talk about
me and you
someday
love poems will apply to us
and Pilipino revolutionaries
will grace the pages of my books
intstead of Shakespeare and Caliban
more than just daydreams
and what if, actually, what if
can you imagine the possibility
that this school
this country
belongs to us

and why don't we
why don't we
take it back
lets take back the morning
take back the breeze
kissing our faces
take back this room and this bed
and let me whisper
I love you
over and over
and let's take back the papers
the headlines
take back the words
the avenue
Philadelphia streets
Mumia and Dylcia
Assata and Marcos
and lets sing
praises to ourselves
let's take back the classes the classrooms
the schools
the liquor stores the tennis courts
let's take it back
all of it
and baby
let's take back this morning
each morning each minute
wrap ourselves in each other
as the curtains kiss us awake
love each other fierce
as warriors tender
as mothers slow

and careful
as revolution.

Qwo-Li Driskill, 22
Glenwood Springs, Colo.

I am a triracial, First Nation, Two-Spirit Fairy Trans Faggot activist. Originally from Glenwood Springs, Colo., I grew up there until I began college in Greeley, Colo., in the fall of 1993. Greeley is very, very conservative. I'm talkin' pre-Stonewall in some ways. The one queer bar was shut down after a police raid.

I came out during the time of Amendment 2 (straight only) and after English-only laws (white only). There is still a lot of anger about A2, regardless of the fact that it was overturned by the Supreme Court. I am quite the Queen, an outspoken survivor of sexual assault and an in-your-face mixed-blood, so I am not safe here at all. But I am committed to speaking out.

I am tired as fuck of our continual dismemberment, erasure, and silencing. I am grateful to my Cherokee, Osage, Delaware, African, and European ancestors for conjuring up this existence. I am committed to unleashing Out/rage/us Acts of Delightful Revolution.

qwo-li driskill

The Memory of Bathing

It was the moment that made us realize why we were there.

My friend Colleen and I, radical queers, AIDS activists, and two strong survivor spirits, were taking in everything we could at the National Lesbian and Gay Health Association Conference and National HIV/AIDS Forum. For days we had been attending important workshops on queer communities and the AIDS crisis. Though disappointed by the underrepresentation of youth and lack of discussion of rural issues, we were both excited to be in Seattle gaining information we had not been exposed to. Each night we would return to our friend Jim's home on Queen Anne Hill, exhausted, and think about the events of the next day.

We were both so overwhelmed. Here we were at a gathering of diverse people with a common goal: to end the decimation of our communities as a result of violence, depression, substance abuse, and AIDS. At a panel of HIV-positive lesbians we stood clapping, moved by the powerful message of these women: "We will not be silent." We heard the words of Terry Tafoya, a Taos Pueblo/Warmsprings Two-Spirit, who spoke about First Peoples, Two-Spirits, and the AIDS plague. This was the first time I had ever met another Native queer, and I whispered *wado* to my ancestors for letting our paths cross.

One night, a symposium was going to run late, so Colleen called Jim to let him know not to expect us before 11 P.M. After making the phone call, Colleen approached me.

"Do you mind if we skip this last symposium?" she asked.

"Well, I really wanted to go...."

"Jim's Chicken Soup client died."

The Chicken Soup Brigade is an organization in Seattle that provides care for people living with AIDS. A moment later we were running through the hallways of the Westin Hotel and maneuvering our way around busses and monorail beams to get to our friend's side.

Jim was in shock. We hugged him and listened to him as he cried. He had planned a visit with his client that day. "I never got to say good-bye to him," he said over and over again. "I bathed him. I've never bathed another person before." Tears made their way down Jim's face in a controlled march.

Colleen and I left the apartment to walk and talk to each other after Jim had gone to sleep. The streets of Seattle were dark and beautiful. Colleen and I talked for hours about how strong and beautiful Jim was and continues to be in fighting the battles he does. We talked about how wondrous it was that we were still alive to be in Seattle with each other, when so often survival seemed unfathomable. We hugged each other tightly, bathing one another in our tears. Goddamnit, we were alive. We had survived. We talked about the awe we had for all our friends, and how Jim stood in utmost stature in our minds. And we wept for Jim. We wept in anger. We wept as an act of resistance against those who will not weep for the loss of our peoples. It was the moment that made us realize why we were there. We were there to weep and to hold each other while we wept. We were there to fight and to find a way out of no way. We were there because we should not be living in a time when one must weep in the memory of bathing another human being.

qwo-li driskill

At the Queer Conference Dinner

I looked into your dark eyes
with shock
when you asked me if I could
do a traditional Indian dance
to entertain these mostly
white faces
All these white faces
except yours and
a few others I could count
on one hand
and I spat out the word
NO
like a rock
hoping its sound falling
to the floor would wake
you up from all these lies
they've fed us
It didn't
I left the room
to stand in the parking
lot and smoke

Brother
How angry I was
for being angry with you
Your young Azteca body
shrouded in the expensive
business clothes
white men wear when they
write out contracts to

sell our grandmothers' hearts
I know you are pleading only
to stay alive
and

One day I will
dance for you
It will be my prayer
that you come home

reate.

Colleen K. Donovan, 20
Olympia, Wash.

I am a student at the Evergreen State College in Olympia, Wash., and am in search of a way to be a writer/activist/revolutionary and get paid enough for survival. A possessor of an alarming cadre of self-chosen labels, I am a Bisexual Youth Activist Advocate Feminist Writer With Cerebral Palsy (using that queer affinity for acronyms, that's BYAAFWWCP). I have discovered that it's my life's work to be a friendly, educational, ANGRY-AS-ALL-HELL advocate for social change.

On Diversity
(Presented at Pride 1997, Olympia, Wash.)

The term *diversity* has become more than trite these days. Slap a rainbow flag on your car and you're well on the way to "diverse" liberalism. A true commitment to diversity, however, requires a closer look at the privileges and oppressions simultaneously affecting each of us and a recognition of both public and private means of resistance. In many ways I have privilege: I am white, middle-class, and attending college. These factors grant me certain societally bestowed benefits. In other ways, I am systemically oppressed: as a woman, as a youth, as a person with cerebral palsy, as a bisexual queer. With these attributes, I fail to meet the optimal requirements for functioning in this white-supremacist, capitalist heteropatriarchy.

If you are not part of the system in the optimal way (i.e., as a straight, white, middle-class or upwardly mobile, Christian male), you pose a threat to that dominant system. For the queer movement to move beyond the notion of "diversity" as just a nice word people use to pay surface attention to or tokenize those who are underrepresented, each of us must live up to and utilize the challenge we present to the system.

As a youth activist, I have seen the systematic devaluation of young people's ideas, thoughts, dreams, musings, and inspirations. Discounted as immature, irresponsible, and ignorant, youth have few rights in this society, and as we have seen with the recent spate of "parental rights" bills, even those few are tenuous. As youth within the queer movement, we challenge that ageist system with our very existence. And it is of utmost importance that queer youth strengthen themselves with a sense of queer his/herstory, find their voices and pave their own way in spite of the many obstacles.

Adult allies of queer youth also challenge that system. Heteropatriarchy is powerful tool that uses scare tactics to separate generations under the myth of "recruitment." Recruitment is a glaring manifestation of the divide-and-conquer maneuver. It is meant to threaten adult allies so that youth are left with little or no adult mentors, resources, or support. Those who recognize this fallacy and remain allies challenge the system by continuing to tell our stories and reclaim our his/herstory across generations. If a people are robbed of their his/herstory, they lose any hope of a collective identity; rob people of their identity and there goes the threat of organized resistance to the status quo. Division is deliberate and strategic. Thus, it is vital we not miss that important link of communication. It's time for us to *talk* to each other about what it means and what it has meant to be queer.

One person can challenge the system in a number of ways: As a bi person, I challenge the either/or nature of human categorization. That is, things tend to be thought of as black or white, man or woman, gay or straight, and as a bi person, all those boxes get rather confining, and things get a bit more gray in regard to gender and sexuality. The challenge to the systems of gender and sexuality that bi and trans people present with their existence can be threatening to both straight and queer communities. Dichotomies, such as those of gender and sexuality, are the root of biphobia, transphobia, and indeed, all oppression. Challenging the hierarchical, dichotomized mind-sets of gender and sexuality is intrinsic to the breakdown of sexism, racism, homo/bi/ and transphobia. As bi and trans people, we must be visible about our subversive identities and utilize the challenge we present to the system—even as we struggle to eradicate bi and transphobia and become an acknowledged and represented part of the queer movement.

In closing, I'd like to address yet another facet of the dynamics of oppression, one that is rarely fully addressed within the queer community or in mainstream society: the dynamic of ableism. Ableism is the systematic devaluation of people with disabilities as "less than human"—perhaps stemming from the subconscious realization of able-bodied folk that they are but one serious injury away from joining our ranks. Again, the sharing of our stories and giving voice to our experiences as "differently abled" individuals is essential. Even as I say the words "differently abled" I am reminded of the awkwardness and silence that surrounds most physical and mental differences. No one word of identification sounds entirely appropriate or comfortable: *disabled, crippled, handicapped, differently abled, lame, dumb, impaired, retarded*. They all reinforce the correlation of physical and mental differences with deficiency. We must work toward breaking our silences and challenging ableism, monosexism, ageism, and all oppressions. With this breaking of silence will come true diversity and inclusion in our movement and beyond.

Beginning Revolutions:
An Interview With Qwo-Li Driskill

If anyone knows about beginning revolutions, it's Qwo-Li Driskill. Driskill is a racially mixed 22-year-old queer Two-Spirit youth activist. His involvement in grassroots rural organizing is impressive and inspirational. He serves as copresident of the Greeley Gay, Lesbian, and Bisexual Alliance, is on the Presidential Task Force for Diversity at the University of Northern Colorado, and works extensively with a number of area organizations, including the Weld County AIDS Coalition, People of the Great Spirit, and Colorado Progressive Coalition.

Colleen: You identify as "Two-Spirit," a term many people may not be familiar with. What does "Two-Spirit" mean to you?

Q-L: I am of racially mixed ancestry: Cherokee, African-American and European, with some Delaware and Osage blood as well. I primarily identify as Cherokee, which is why I use the term "Two-Spirit." It provides a way for me to reclaim what it means to be what European culture defines as bi, gay, lesbian, and transgender (BGLT) within a Cherokee/Native American context. BGLT refers strictly to sexual orientation. The term "Two-Spirit" indicates more of a way of perception, of living life as a border-crosser, a person in balance, living between the worlds of male/female, flesh/spirit. BGLT also implies genders, when in Native culture genders are not polarized. In some tribes there are as many as six genders. It's a much more all-encompassing, inclusive term within my own context.

C: How has being racially mixed affected your life?

Q-L: It's been very dismembering. In this white-supremacist culture, there is no place for racially mixed people to fit in. It creates a conflict for me, which has been mirrored for generations by my ancestors. My European ancestors enslaved both Cherokee and African-Americans. My Cherokee ancestors enslaved my African-American ancestors. The Cherokee and the Osage were at war before the Trail of Tears, and currently the Delaware are trying to secede from the Cherokee Nations. The history of genocide in this country has created constant conflict for racially mixed folk.

C: Has this helped you in becoming an activist?

Q-L: I come from lots of marginalizing experiences. I grew up poor, racially mixed, and I am a survivor of sexual assault. Becoming an activist, for me, was a way of survival. I had to speak out, because I felt if I didn't say something, no one else would. If we don't vocalize our own experiences, it's part of our own demise. In addition to vocalizing ourselves we need to listen to each other, because a queer movement that does not fight all "isms" (racism, sexism, classism, ableism) with equal emphasis will not succeed. People of color are not acknowledged as an integral part of the queer movement; we're not given space or recognition within the queer media; we're tokenized at conferences. It's not enough for the movement to "listen" to people of color, we should have our own rightful place within the mainstream movement, which is still being run by upper–middle-class, white gay men. If you don't fight for women's rights, then you're only fighting for the rights of gay/bi men; if you don't fight racism, you're assuming all queers are white; the list goes on. All oppression is so linked, you can't fight it without fighting all of it. Queers who are racist and sexist need to get out of the way. We don't have time for them anymore.

C: Speaking of "isms," have you run into ageism as a queer youth activist?

Q-L: On the whole, particularly within the mainstream queer media, queer youth and elders are ignored and devalued. This is one of the weakest aspects of our movement—little to no intergenerational communication. Youth today are coming out in junior high and high school; we're dealing with whole new issues. We've grown up with AIDS, and we've never known a time without it. It's highly irresponsible for queer adults to ignore queer youth, because youth started our movement. What I've run into is adults wanting to speak for youth. Adults need to realize that no one knows the experiences of queer youth but youth themselves. We come from myriad experiences, which, when we loosen our tongues, can begin revolutions.

C: Do you have any advice for queer youth who may have trouble "loosening their tongues"?

Q-L: Love yourself. Respect yourself. Take care of yourselves and each other, because all we have is each other. One of the major barriers to empowerment of all queer youth is divisiveness and pettiness among ourselves, which is exactly what dominant culture wants. If we're divided, we can't work for change, and our systematic erasure continues. Being unabashedly out is one of the most important political statements a queer youth can make. We need to realize our own power, that our voices are just as valid and important as anyone else's. We can't back down. If we're ignored or tokenized, we have to fight even harder and louder.

reate.

Bree Zuckerman, 21 Olean, N.Y.

I am a queer-identified 21-year-old from western New York State, now living in Brooklyn. I use writing to engage and negotiate with the world. This poem was written in a moment in which the words were moving furiously in the space between my thoughts and the world around me. I wrote it in October 1998 after being a part of a peaceful action in New York City intended to honor Matthew Shepard and resist the hatred and violence that allow racist/sexist/homophobic violence to continue. The NYPD responded to the crowd with divisive tactics and outright brutality. I wrote this to try to make sense of that night and to explore what direction we as a community should head next.

October 20

last night they came for 400 and
we answered them
tenfold
taking four city blocks
as our own
breathing resistance back
into the lungs of
new york city.

i look up now
at the buildings
impossibly tall standing
midtown hardened
against the sunlight
and i know last night
we coulda
humbled them with our strength.
last night
we coulda
made them crumble
with the weight
a collective
anger.

we coulda
made them topple
even as we were caught beneath
hooves between
fists against
concrete bleeding

'cuz we asked for too much
'cuz we asked that the world
sit up and take notice
on account of our dying
on account of demanding
the freedom
to love.

and they
standing stiffstraightscared
that we might be onta something
and began speaking in tongues of hate
their ears deaf to bones
splintering like glass.

last night we filled the veins
of the city so that it
may live again.
last night we (were) moved
for the boy
who died
nakedbruisedbleeding
on a fencepost.
for the nameless brown boys
beaten on the way home.

last night we (were) moved
for those whose voices have been
absored
by the neverending machinery
whose stories don't reach
our tired ears.

the black the brown the poor the trans
bodies buried
every day.

we were a mouth like a gaping wound
for the screams
so long coming

and i wonder on this quiet workweek morning

where is that rage?

where is the rage
        that for a moment
                cracked this city open
                        and left it raw,
                                bleeding?

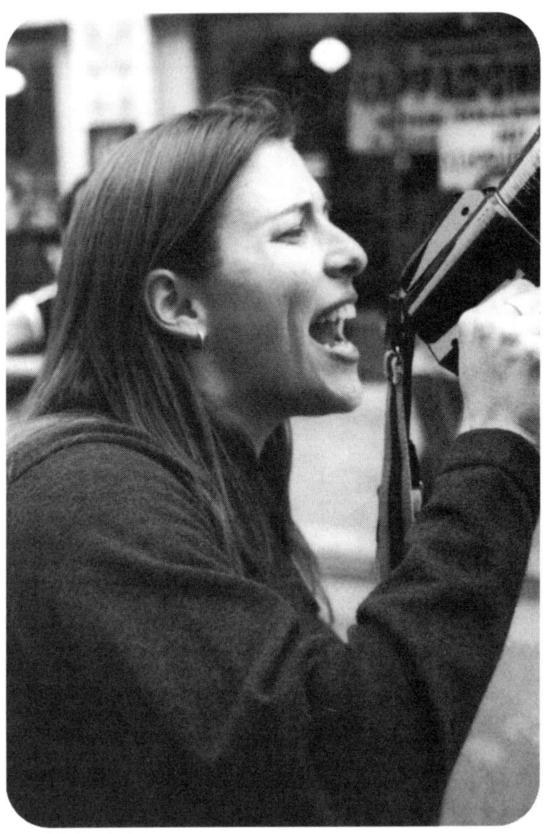

María Poblet, 22
Oakland, Calif.

I am a 22-year-old Latina trying to become a revolutionary and trying to figure out how cultural work could contribute to a revolution in this country. I am an organizer and a poetry teacher (not that I can tell those two occupations apart).

nothing is more cruel

after my father names
me
his shame
i hang up shaking
then try to pray louder than the dial tone

guerrilla poetry manifesto

today we starve two hundred Iraqi children
today we bomb Kosovars from their homes
but i can't find the words against sanctions
can't find words to explain the missile-bruised sky

and today uc berkeley bureaucrats slash ethnic studies
but i can't find the words to speak for my people
can't find the words to speak for myself

so today i resolve to write guerrilla poems
to aim words against bureaucrats and their bombs
learn to clear my head in a bart train or on a street corner
learn to write faster than cruise missiles fall

i will learn the discipline of a guerrilla poet
sleep lightly with a pen at my side
i will learn to write guerrilla poems
and launch them like molotov cocktails

i must invent the words i cannot find
because today survival takes a verse
and tomorrow survival takes an AK
i will learn the strategy of war

Lisa Lusero, 23
Denver, Colo.

I am a proud lifelong resident of Colorado, living in Denver and born and raised in Boulder County. I am committed to fighting for the silenced and underheard in this community and beyond. I came into my queerness at a small liberal arts university in the Northwest that wasn't exactly queer-friendly but allowed enough of us meet and work our hearts out to make it so. I claim *queer* not only as a sexual identity but as a political position. I want to always stand on the edges looking for the places that don't quite fit, listening to the people who aren't really seen, and standing up for every Other I can find.

Impossible Body is a one-woman performance piece I wrote and perform. In it I weave personal stories about my life as a shaven-headed Chicana lesbian with the voices and stories of some other characters moving within my impossible body. The following are excerpts from the script.

Excerpts From *Impossible Body*

Space 1

You're the woman from my dreams. This is incredible. I've been having these dreams about this woman who follows me everywhere, trying to explain herself to me—but she can't. And every time I wake up I think I should tell her not to be scared, I should tell her it's OK, that she can tell me everything. And it's you. You're her. Don't be scared.

Space 2

I just kept falling in love with women; it wouldn't stop. So I realized I'm a lesbian. But then I was a lesbian trying to be in a monogamous relationship. And I still kept falling in love with women.

Finally, I had to realize that I'm a polyamorous lesbian! Yes, it's a word. Polyamorous. Loving many all at one time!

Space 4

Don't bother looking at me it doesn't make any sense
I've got no problem with my body
it's just always been surprising that I only have one.
Don't tell me about identity, I've got plenty.
No sense in siphoning off selves,
I'm just trying to salvage what I've got—
a little too much of everything in this one me.
Such a little body, such a silly face,
such an impossible posture to position.
No matter how hard I try I can't match the insides to the outsides,
I can't make my hips any wider than they are,

can't make my lip curl just right or my eyelashes fall just so
and I still have dreams of myself with long flowing hair
a purple hue and bright red lips waiting to kiss.

Space 5

I learned the truth about Santa Claus and masturbation in the same year. I was 9. I had a hunch about Santa, but I had no clue about masturbation. I mean, I had no clue there was anything wrong with it. As far as I know, I've been masturbating my whole life. But it wasn't until 9 that I realized it was an impulse that you had to turn off. Especially in class. Fourth grade craft time taught me shame. The truth about Santa Claus could hardly compare.

Space 7

Allison and I met freshman year of college. We lived in the same dorm and each had three roommates. Little did I know I was already desperately in love. Little did she know—until I kissed her. I was out of my mind. I said something like, "The lips of my soul touch your face, the lips of my soul soft upon your face, I see, I understand. Do you?"

And she said "No," just as a single tear trickled down her cheek and fell onto my lip.

Space 8

Maybe I should explain this polyamorous thing—I fell in love with a woman in the grocery store. Our eyes locked as we passed each other in the dry goods aisle, and I felt like a large gong struck the side of my head. I encountered another woman waiting in line, we exchanged glances, she smiled. I immediately believed she was an angel sent down to deliver a message to my soul. There is a piece of me lost in every woman I meet. She holds a secret about me I long to know.

Space 12

When I was 16, I was so scared I might be gay, but I didn't know how to tell. So I went to the library and I typed in: G-A-Y. I was hoping to find some manual on how to know if you're gay, like a book of symptoms or something. All I found was a scientific study on homosexuality in cows.

Which I read.

Apparently cows are gay too.

But that wasn't comforting at the time.

Space 16

Maybe I should explain this polyamorous thing. See, language betrays me.

Hi. This is my, uh, friend Allison.

Hi. This is my, roommate, Allison.

This is my lover.

This is my wife.

My companion.

My partner.

This is my partner, Allison.

I get one word, a word that barely fits as it is, to describe the big, huge love in my life. And that one word has been taken now for several years. But what about the other loves?

Hi, this is the woman who woke the sleeping giant of erotic

energy within me and reminded me I could only hide from my passions for so long.

This is my, uh, friend.

And what about the woman who held up a mirror with her body for my own sexuality to be reflected in?

What can I call her? Hi, this is my really supergood friend!

What words can I use so that we all understand what I mean? How can I speak at all when I am trapped by so many words that lie?

Space 18

Sometimes I am desperately attracted to men. I feel crazy for sex with them, but then I feel ugly and cruel. Like an unruly beast; selfish and despicable. I have loved many men with my heart. And I have wanted many men with my body. But I have never loved and wanted a man at the same time.

My desire for men feels like an unbalanced teeter-totter. I love him. I want him. I love him. I want him. I spent a large portion of my adolescence on this dilemma. Meanwhile, my desire for women rose up out of my love until they were moving as one. I love you, I want you, I love you, I want you.

When Allison and I finally made love everything fell into place. The sexual monster inside turned into a band of purple fairy dust, and I could fly. Touching her felt like worship, like running my hands along the majestic robes of God. I cried. When she touched me my heart rose from somewhere dark and broke into waves at the touch of light. Somehow she knew where to find me, somehow she put my pieces back together and carried me home.

Sex and gender are tied up in very complicated knots, and for some reason I don't understand, with women my sexuality feels whole.

Of course, I haven't run tests on every man, every woman. This lesbian thing—it's not truth, it's just a trend.

A *very* persistent trend...

That's how we exist—trusting trends, building truth. For all I know I could find myself one day loving a man like I love women—and if that happens, I'll simply revise the label and move on. There are no rules, just the unmistakable force of human heat.

Space 17

I never thought I was confused about my gender until I realized gender was confused with me. Cut my hair, and suddenly it's, "Sir! Sir!" And I can't tell you how many children have come up to me and asked, "Are you a boy or a girl?"

One kid even argued with me.

It was summer, I was wearing a baggy T-shirt, shorts and a baseball cap. This kid came up to me and challenged, "How old are you?"

I was 20 at the time. But he didn't believe me. So I got out my driver's license to impress him. At which point the situation became perfectly clear.

"That's not you," he said, "that's a girl."

Aha! He noticed my adolescent boy drag.

"I am a girl!" I said, and pulled a gender trump card, illustrating my breasts.

"Then why do you have hair on your legs?"

"It grows there," I said, "and anything that tells you otherwise is a lie."

"You're no girl."

There was no convincing him. I simply lacked proper identification.

And ever since that happened, I've realized it is rather confusing, "Are you a boy or a girl?" I mean, who gets to decide, you or me?

Space 19

Sometimes I imagine myself the white, middle-aged, suburban mother of two. I want to be beautiful. So I Jazzercise. I want a nice home. I keep a garden in the yard. I want grandkids. I want to spoil little grandkids. I want to take their darling pictures and show them to all my friends. I want my daughter to be someone I recognize. A friend.

Space 20

One courageous evening I read a section of my journal to my freshman roommate:

"When I look at myself in the mirror, I don't know who it is."

I was hoping on some level she would see through my thinly veiled plea and summon forth all my deeply hidden secrets. But I guess reading that summoned forth all of her deeply hidden secrets. And suddenly she said, "I've never told this to anyone before," and the stories started tumbling forth as she tried to look that African-American face in the mirror and know, almost every time, who she was.

Trying to match the insides with the outsides. Betrayed by skin as I was betrayed by gender, sex. Realizing together that some boxes just don't fit. Some lies escape unnoticed. Some rage can't be reconciled alone.

She never had to say, "Are you gay?" We both knew. And I just said, "Yes, it's true." Even though I barely understood what that meant. Just as she barely understood what the fact that her boyfriend was white meant. What the fact that her hair was straightened meant. What the history of her name meant. We barely understood, and yet we were fighting to crawl out of those boxes and communicate something from our individual betrayals. Something bigger than skin and bones.

What we managed to communicate was that racism and homophobia come from the same human impulse to run away from the unknown. What we managed to understand is that we were both suffering from that terrible human recognition of being the run-from.

Space 21

I want to throw my pain out with my voice. I want to show my rage on my face, I want to block your fatal blow, I want to move on, I want to stay back, I want to learn something new, I want to never know again. I want to explain this feeling in my chest like shattering glass from my shoulders to my hands. I'm scared and it makes my heart go up in my throat and it makes my sides full and it makes my ears ring and it makes my ears ring and it makes me choke.

Space 22

Sometimes I imagine myself as a U.S. Senator. I wear a large, proud grin as the wrinkles on my face collect rivulets of sweat. My round, stalky body pushes at the seams of my blue suit, but I fit comfortably in my space. *I want to make life better for you and for your family. The very foundations of our society are in danger of being burned. The flames of hedonism, the flames of narcissism, the flames of self-centered morality are licking at the very foundations of our society—the family unit. The courts in Hawaii have rendered a decision loud and clear. They have told the lower court: You will recognize same-sex marriages. What more does it take, America? Enough is enough. We must maintain a moral foundation, an ethical foundation for our families and ultimately for the United States of America. I want to protect your world. And mine.*[1]

Space 23

I want to protect your world. And mine.

Space 24

OK, I'll admit it. I cut my hair because I wanted people to know I was a dyke. I may be breaking some lesbian code of silence by admitting this. I think we're supposed to pretend that our haircuts happen independent of our sexuality, and for some this may be true. But for me there is a direct connection. I am conscious of my sexuality all the time, and I don't want it hiding under a conventional 'do. Passing for straight makes me feel invisible. And I hate that. I want to be seen clearly and explicitly for who I am.

Don't assume your world is mine.

Then again, don't assume it isn't.

Space 25

the problem is not
that i am in love with too many people
though i am
the problem is that i only have one body
to do the loving in

Space 26

Sometimes I imagine myself with long black hair, dark skin to match the Chicana in me, and long nails painted red. I wear a tight leather skirt to tempt you, and I am full of power and controlled desire. I stand back, watching you watch me, weaving fantasies before your eyes. *¿Hablas español? Necessito una persona con la lengua, con las palabras.*

If I had words, I could speak. If I just had the words, I could weave fantasies before your eyes. But this woman doesn't know how to speak. I'm caught. Trapped in a confused body. I am the Chicana woman. *¡Soy Lusero! ¿Entiendes? Soy Lusero.* I feel sexy, full of power and controlled desire. I feel like the spider woman weaving fantasies before your eyes.

But I don't match.

Last fall I was invited to a reception for graduate students of color. When I arrived the woman at the door promptly told me, "There's a reception here right now."

"I know."

"Did you receive an invitation?"

Needless to say, the evening didn't have the warm air of camaraderie I had hoped.

Something in my skin lied. See, they didn't know that hidden beneath this ivory white skin is a real Chicana woman, a real woman of color—right? They couldn't see Grandma Lusero marching under my skin to Spanish Mass. They couldn't hear in my ears the drunk-slurred, "Hey wetback, where's your fuckin' green card?" as my uncles almost launched into a barroom brawl. They couldn't see my beautiful, brown-skinned cousin Sylvia, whom I've been in love with all my life. And they couldn't see Gilberto sitting there behind my eyes, Dr. Lusero, relegated to the empty wing of a hotel when they realized Lusero was a dirty Mexican and not the doctor they expected to greet.

They couldn't see beneath my skin to this real Chicana lesbian woman who doesn't know how to be anymore brown, who doesn't know how to be any less lesbian, *y que no sabe como hablar más español.* They couldn't see beneath my skin—and sometimes neither can I.

So as a student of color, I left that reception with one solid lesson: Race doesn't make any more sense than sex.

Space 27

Sometimes I feel too wise.

The kind of wisdom that comes from seeing a broken heart in your mother's eyes.

My Mom was sexually abused as a child. Her hurt was born into me. I know. Her scars lie beneath my skin. This is the pain I always see; there are far too many faces like hers with shadows of abuse. Shadows falling even across the strongest faces. Which hurts the most. Seeing in a second that wide chasm between a powerful presence and a terrified soul. Between the mom taking care of me and the little girl who was raped.

Space 32

Don't bother looking at me, it just doesn't make sense
I can't summon the goddess to take shape
I can't pull the moon from my fingertips or wrap a rainbow
    around your heart
I can't dance without legs or stand while flying
or battle without armor or sing without a face.
I've got no problem with my body, it's just always been
    surprising that I only have one.

Space 34

Sometimes I imagine myself round, like the Earth. Big hips and inviting breasts flowing over my chest. I am draped in bright colors of soft fabric and every move I make flows with the ease of the wind. I sit strong and gather you into my comforting arms, where I hold you and tell you tales with a dark, honey-flavored voice that dips and spins and whispers and hums. There is a long history to your beauty. Rising out of me like tears from a fallen forest weeping your return. Baby, you were once my child. Born like a sun bolt dancing. Your fire turned laughter into sky. Your loving turned water into song. There is a long history to your beauty, baby. Swollen and arching, knees deep, wide moaning and praying. You were once my bride. Flowing through me like hot sand crawling to the sea. Baby, I know the history of your beauty. 'Cause you were once me. And I feel your embrace like memory.

Space 35

(She approaches the nearest audience member.) You were in my dream last night, walking alone. And in that moment, I loved you, completely. I figure your solitude can't be that much different from mine. Don't be scared.

Space 36

I want to explain this polyamorous thing....

But I can't.

I think I've slipped off the cultural map. I can't point to where I'm at, or give directions from the highway. I'm looking for a language that's not here yet.

Except here's an analogy: We've got this flame and we want to share it.

I've noticed when we do there's more light.

Space 37

"K-Sig's kick butt!" "I love to suck dick." "Jesus died for our sins." "God hates fags."

There I was again—reading library-desk graffiti. (Now to the audience)

"Pot is my god." "Praise god and fuck me." "Why are you reading this?" "Erica gives good head." "Lesbians lick pussy and go to hell." "Help—I think this might be me." (pause) Lesbians lick pussy—Help. (pause) I think this might be me.

Suddenly this scared lesbian voice struck me—Help. Scrawled

there in our most public forum for the honest exchange of opinions. I think this might be me.

So I left my name and number. I know—stupid, crazy. I'm asking for trouble. But if not me—who? Is this woman going to find wisdom and guidance from a K-Sig pothead, or Erica the amazing cocksucker? So I took a chance. "I can help. Lisa—761-9074, call me." That night Allison answered the phone. And when I got there—nothing but that painfully empty dial tone. Allison said it was a girl. She sounded scared. And I knew it was her. From the desk. I just hoped she'd get the courage up to try again.

I visited the desk again the next day. She wrote, "Sorry about the phone call. I'm chickenshit. Maybe I'll try again. Thanks."

"Yes! Try again!," I wrote. "Or just write here. I want to help you. You'll be OK."

The next time I came to the desk she drew an arrow—down. OK? I looked all over for another clue. And finally, crumpled up in a corner underneath the desk, I found a note.

"I felt bad about defacing the desk," she wrote. So our conversations moved to paper. I left her the call number to an obscure book I felt confident would be left alone. And we stashed our correspondence there. It was Gertrude Stein's *Geography and Plays*, by the way. I didn't think Gertrude would mind.

My first letter was desperate. I didn't know where this woman was—whether she was near suicide or just looking for a friend. So I rattled off hot line numbers, book suggestions, support groups, and encouragement: "You're OK. You're not alone. You're courageous for just reaching out. You're gonna make it. It gets better from here."

She was beyond the initial "My god, I might be gay." And was more in need of a friend, a voice. She asked me about myself. And apologized for not leaving her name.

"My parents did not bless me with a name that would allow me to hide in the masses," she said.

And I tried to imagine what that name might be as I began to tell her my story, to tell her anything and everything about me just to give her a real, live lesbian being to hold onto—if only in her mind. I drew her a stick-figure picture of myself. In case we should pass someday in the library, I wanted her to be able to watch me, see me exist in body. Even if she never approached.

Her trust grew through the letters. I suggested we meet. And in her next letter she said, "Yeah, I think I'd like to meet you too." She described the Rasta backpack she always carried and the black cap she always wore. She left me her number and for the first time, signed her name. Ebony. I shook my head as her race bled through the letters of her name, and I understood the nature of her multiple invisibilities. Race and sexuality colliding again.

We met. And talked and shared more stories with each other. I introduced her to my partner, my friends. She reminded me of the importance of visibility, the complexities of race and sexuality. I gave her a copy of my lesbian magazine with a beautiful Black dyke on the cover. She gave me another story to tell.

Now I never underestimate the writing on the walls. Behind every anonymous "I love to suck dick" or "God hates fags" is a real, live body with a real, live story to tell. When we finally talked, the anonymous "Help" turned into a Black lesbian Rasta woman and that terrifying phone number transformed into me.

If it takes the anonymity of library desk graffiti to finally meet, I am willing to wait. Because these bodies are proof of a beautiful and hard-won existence. Our stories are something powerful to share.

Space 38

I can feel the rush of everything moving in and stretching across my body.

It feels so good to touch
my warmth to your warmth
living breathing dancing alive

It feels so good
to move
to run and jump and laugh and cry and pray and try and wish and scream and sew the stars into the sky
It isn't about sex, really, it's about finding joy.

i welcome this light

i welcome the sun the air the growing trees

i welcome a silence a peace a slowness

i welcome my own power my own poet my own time

i welcome limits and depths and possibilities

and i give thanks

in this impossible body

I feel

joy!

Space 39

Sometimes I imagine the Suburban Mother and the Butch Dyke could get along. Sometimes I imagine the Wispy Woman on the Bus and the Sexy Chicana falling in love. Sometimes I imagine Round Like the Earth singing lullabies to a U.S. Senator.

Sometimes I imagine…

Space 40

…you've been in my dreams. And I think I need to tell you: It's all right if you feel scared; just don't get stuck there. OK?

[1]The U.S. senator's speech was inspired by a quote from Rep. Bob Barr (R-Georgia).

reate.

queer 101: a glossary

Welcome to our glossary of some terms relevant to the lives, politics, and creative work of queer youth. Many are terms used by the writers in this book; some are words or phrases used in queer communities, the academy, or by activists. These definitions are not meant to be comprehensive. They were written by some of this book's contributors based on conversations, books we've read, and life experiences. They are meant to be expanded, challenged, and redefined.

Ableism: The exclusion of people with physical and/or developmental impairments from social, economic, and political power. This is supported by the assumption of superiority by those who consider themselves able-bodied. (See *discrimination, oppression, prejudice, power.*)

Adultism: The oppression of youth or children in which age is used as a basis for discrimination, abuse, or deprivation of basic rights and freedoms (economic, emotional, political, etc.). This is sometimes referred to as paternalism, in which adults' guidance or discipline of youth undermines our basic human rights. Queer youth are acutely affected by this, for instance, when adults assume our sexuality/gender identity is a "phase" or subject us to therapy aimed at making us straight. (See *discrimination, oppression, prejudice, power.*)

Ageism: Discrimination against a person/group based on actual or perceived age. Most often directed at youth or the elderly. (See *discrimination, oppression, prejudice, power.*)

Ambisexual: Of all sexes or sexually attracted to persons of any sex. Defined in this way, ambisexual can be applied to gender identity or sexuality.

Androgyny: Displaying characteristics of both or neither of the two culturally defined genders.

Binary: A system of likes and opposites. Binaries arrange people and things into opposing categories. This relates to the queer community in that a binary system separates men/women, gay/straight, masculine/feminine and pits us against one another. It means we're assigned to one or the other and aren't supposed to be both or neither. (See *gender regime.*)

Biphobia: Hatred and/or discrimination against bisexuals. Like *transphobia*, this form of discrimination comes from both the straight and gay community. The straight community often collapses bisexuality into homosexuality and refers to bi people as "gay." Thus, bisexuals face the same forms of job, housing, and medical discrimination, difficulty in adopting children, discharge from the military, and emotional and physical violence. The gay/lesbian community, on the other hand, often discriminates against bisexuals for being able to "pass" as straight or for being "confused." (See also *binary, discrimination*.)

Bisexual: A person who is emotionally, spiritually, physically, and/or sexually attracted to those of any sex or gender.

Black triangle: Though the *pink triangle* is a widely recognized symbol of queer identity and rights, the pink triangle was originally used in the concentration camps of Nazi Germany to identify gay men ("sexual deviants") and *not* lesbian women. Lesbian women were given a black triangle, the symbol of asexuals, because Hitler's regime did not recognize the validity of lesbian sexuality. Today, both men and women wear the pink triangle to show support for queer causes or to identify themselves as queer, but it is important to know the history of the symbols so we do not collapse lesbianism into gay male sexuality.

Classism: The dominance of those with more money and/or power over those with less money and/or power. In capitalist societies this manifests itself in the false idea that the rich are somehow better than the poor and are entitled to exploit poor people's land and labor. It also means that low-income individuals are disregarded and blamed for their own oppression. Many factors contribute to class oppression and status, including age, race, sex, gender, sexuality, ability, education level, and nationality. (See also *discrimination, oppression, white supremacy, ageism, ableism, sexism.*)

Coming out: The process of realizing, understanding, and accepting one's sexual or gender identity. This usually involves telling others. Because it's a process, coming out isn't a one-time deal. It happens each time you present yourself as nonstraight. Because we live in a *heterosexist* society, straight people don't usually have to come out.

Compulsory heterosexuality: A "man-made institution," as poet and theorist Adrienne Rich calls it, that pervades our cultures, telling us women are innately attracted only to men and men are innately attracted only to women. This idea is upheld by the bombardment of heterosexual images in the media and cultural assumptions that everyone's straight. It invalidates queer identities and makes many queer people invisible. This is why you never hear about someone coming out as straight.

Deconstruct: To take apart, break down, or look critically at systems and, in doing so, determine what makes them up and how to effectively change them.

Discrimination: A behavior that results in different and unequal treatment of an individual or community based on their perceived social group (age, race, class, sex, gender, sexuality, ability, etc). Discrimination = behavior. (See *prejudice*.)

Drag: Wearing the clothing of another gender, often exaggerating stereotypical characteristics of that gender.

Dyke: Historically, this term has been an insult used against women perceived to be lesbian or "masculine," similar to butch, she-male, bulldyke, bulldagger, lezzie, etc. Some queers have reclaimed the word as a way to identify and empower themselves. Reclaiming words in this way is often a political act and a tool for empowerment. (See also *fag* and *queer*.)

Fag: Historically this term has been an insult used against men perceived to be homosexual or "feminine," similar to sissy, pussy, pansy, punk, fairy, queer, etc. Some queers have reclaimed the word as a way to identify and empower themselves. Reclaiming words in this way is often a political act and a tool for empowerment. (See also *dyke* and *queer*.)

FTM: Female to Male. A term used in the queer community that refers to male-identified persons who were categorized as female at birth. (See also *MTF* and *transgender*.)

Gay: A person who identifies as a man who is emotionally, spiritually, physically and/or sexually attracted primarily to other men. *Gay*, however, is often used as an umbrella term for both same-gender–loving men and women, and many women identify as gay rather than, or in addition to, *lesbian.*

Gender: Characteristics of masculinity and femininity that are learned or chosen. A person's assigned sex does not always match their gender (see *transgender*), and most people display traits of more than one gender. Gender is also different from *sexuality.*

Gender bending: Messing with stereotypical gender roles. Sometimes referred to as *genderfuck.*

Gender regime: A gender regime dictates that there are only two genders and regulates what it means to be a boy or a girl, a man or a woman. (See *binary*.) The idea is that males should be masculine and females should be feminine. A gender regime informs our understandings of our bodies, our "roles," and the punishments that come with challenging those roles. A gender regime has built-in controls to keep us in our assigned roles, such as the threat of violence, ridicule, or rejection and the lack of models for anything different. A gender regime is policed and upheld by *heterosexism* and *patriarchy*.

Hegemony: Here's a word academics like to use a lot to sound smart, but it's actually a pretty useful term. Hegemony is invisible and/or unrecognized forces of power that oppress, restrict, or limit certain groups or individuals.

Heteropatriarchy: A big but useful term that describes the way in which heterosexuality and *patriarchy* (a structure in which men dominate) work together to shape and mandate oppressions. Working together, heterosexuality and patriarchy are made to seem like the "natural" order of things. The term is a good way to draw attention to the ways oppressions function together. As Suzanne Pharr states, "Homophobia is a weapon of sexism," and vice versa.

Heterosexism: The belief that heterosexuality is superior to other sexual orientations. Sort of like straight supremacy. It is one of the central ideas behind homo-, bi-, and transphobia and is key to maintaining *patriarchy*. (See also *oppression, prejudice, power*.)

Homophobia: Hatred and/or discrimination based on perceived or actual sexuality or gender identity. Homophobia manifests itself in a variety of ways, including verbal threats, jokes, physical violence, and discrimination in adoption, marriage, employment, and so on. (See also *discrimination* and *internalized homophobia*.)

Homosociality: This term refers to the bond between same-sex persons that may or may not develop into a sexual attraction; it recognizes the potential or capacity for same-sex love.

Ideology: Beliefs we learn and/or ascribe to. Sometimes we consider them our personal beliefs even though we learn them from dominant society (e.g., racism, homophobia, sexism, ableism, classism, etc). Ideologies are shaped and upheld by *institutions*.

Institutions: Big, bad things. No, just kidding. Institutions are those structures in which most government and societal power are invested. Marriage is an institution in which a lot of religious, social, and economic power is invested. Education is another institution that is often given less money, but is powerful in shaping or attempting to shape our young minds. Institutions are the structures that help form and uphold *ideologies*.

Internalize: To take upon oneself images or ideas invented by others. To internalize another's opinion of you is to allow them to define who you are.

Internalized homophobia: A hatred or fear of your own existing or potential homosexuality. It is largely responsible for the staggering numbers of queer teen suicides, depression, and substance abuse. It is also a contributing factor in violence against those perceived to be queer. Internalized ableism, biphobia, racism, sexism, and transphobia, likewise, are responsible for shame, negative body image, and violence within our communities. Though the word *internalize* sounds negative, it is possible to internalize positive self-images and pride.

Intersexed: Describes people born multisexed (born with some combination of male and female sex organs). According to the Intersex Society of North America, "Anatomic sex differentiation occurs on a male/female continuum, and there are several dimensions." It is estimated that anywhere from 1 in 100 to 1 in 2,000 infants is born intersexed, but the most common reaction by the medical establishment is to "fix" these babies immediately. Many consider "fixing" intersexed infants mutilation.

Kinsey Scale: The model devised by Alfred Kinsey in 1948 that plotted sexuality on a scale from 0 to 6—0 being exclusively heterosexual and 6 exclusively homosexual. According a 1954 survey using the scale, 70% of people feel between 1-5, making it the first linear scale to account for bisexuality. It's been criticized, though, for being too linear and only accounting for behaviors, not for gender identity.

Lesbian: A person who identifies as a woman who is emotionally, spiritually, physically and/or sexually attracted primarily to other women.

LGBTQ: Lesbian, Gay, Bisexual, Transgender, Questioning/ Queer. Also LGBTI to include intersexed folks or GLBTQ, BGLT, etc.

Monosexism: Privileging a single-gender orientation over trans or bi identities. Monosexism mandates that we be attracted to only one gender, that we "act out" or display characteristics of only one gender.

MTF: Male to Female. A term used in the queer community that refers to female-identified persons who were categorized as male at birth. (See also *FTM* and *transgender*.)

Norms (with regard to sex and gender): The assumptions about sex, sexuality and gender that are taught from the time we're children.

Omnisexual (pansexual): Broadly defined, someone who is emotionally, spiritually, physically, and/or sexually attracted to those of all genders or sexes.

Oppression: The use of power and the effects of domination. Around the world, prejudice + power = oppression. (See also *ableism, ageism, classism, heterosexism, racism*, and *sexism*.)

Pansexual: See *omnisexual*.

Passing: With regard to sex, gender, and sexuality, being (mis)read as a sex, gender, or sexuality other than the one you were assigned or identify with.

Patriarchy: Literally, the "rule of the father," this is the system of male supremacy and power dominant in most cultures around the world. Patriarchy is integrally linked to other oppressive systems such as white supremacy, heterosexism, capitalism, and imperialism.

Pink triangle: The pink triangle (worn point down) has become a symbol of gay rights and identity, like the rainbow flag, often worn by our allies as well by queers. The symbol was appropriated from Nazi Germany where perceived homosexuals were among the first forced into concentration camps and among the millions murdered under Hitler's regime. The pink triangle was used to mark gay men the way the yellow triangle/star was used to denote Jewish men and women. Though it is a widely recognized symbol for gay and lesbian identity, the pink triangle was used to identify only gay *men*. A *black triangle*, the symbol of asexuals, was used to denote lesbian women.

Political: The term *political*, as used in this book, incorporates both traditional government politics and the development of personal politics that happen on an individual or community level. Being political means making sense out of the world around you and looking critically at mainstream ideas. Politics aren't just about upper-middle class white guys in suits with campaign posters. It's more extensive than that. Being yourself in a world that tries to make you like everyone else is political. Coming out can be a political act. Or as 23-year-old Lisa Lusero explains in her bio for this book, we can claim queerness as both a sexual identity and a political position. Within this book, the term implies a critical understanding of the world and a desire for social change.

Polyamory: Loving many at one time. Usually used to refer to nonmonogamous relationships.

Power: Control, access, and influence. Having power means having legitimate *control of* or *access to* resources and having the power to define/influence who else can access those resources. Legitimate power = legal power, specially granted to some and withheld from others. (See *privilege* and *prejudice*.)

Prejudice: A prejudgment in favor of or against a person/group, often based on stereotypes. Prejudice = attitudes. Prejudice + power = oppression. (See *discrimination, power, oppression*.)

Privilege: A right, favor, immunity, or advantage specially granted to one individual or group and withheld from another.

Queer: An umbrella term for lesbian, gay, bisexual, transgender, and intersexed folks. Also, someone who self-identifies as part of the LGBTI community and makes a *political choice* to align themselves outside of heteronorms. Historically, the term has been used as an insult against those perceived to be LGBTI. For this reason its use today is controversial. It was reclaimed in the '80s by a group called Queer Nation, and has since been embraced by many who are antiassimilationist and recognize the sexual and gender diversity of our community.

Racism: Racial prejudice + power. Racism is an ideology that has been deeply ingrained into our cultures, our subconscience, and the institutions around us. (See also *white supremacy, oppression, prejudice, power*.)

(Assigned) Sex: The biological traits used to categorize someone as either male or female. Not all people are born one or the other. (See *intersexed*.) The meaning we impose on sex is called *gender*.

Sexism: A system of discrimination against and exploitation of women based on the ideology of male supremacy. (See also *patriarchy, oppression, prejudice, power*.)

Sexual identity: How you identify your sexual preferences, not necessarily your practices.

Sexuality: Who you like and what you do. Sexuality is distinct from gender identity and sex. It refers to the labels we assign to sexual desires and practices: homosexual, heterosexual, bisexual, ambisexual, asexual, omnisexual, etc.

S/he: A pronoun used in place of she or he (terms used in a *binary* gender system) when you want to talk about someone whose gender doesn't neatly fit into a particular box. (See also *ze*.)

S/M (sadomasochism): There are varying definitions of S/M, especially in relation to queer youth. For the purposes of this book though, S/M is defined as the consensual exchange of power between partners involving the use of pain, domination, or submission to achieve pleasure. S/M is practiced in both heterosexual and queer relationships including activities such as whipping, bondage, fisting, role playing, spanking, and paddling. It is important to note that a nonconsensual sexual act should not be excused as S/M. It is abuse. It is also very important to educate yourself about S/M activity and safety before participating in it.

Stereotype: A negative prejudgment or generalization about a group based on an individual characteristic, which may or may not be based in reality. Some common stereotypes include: Gay men are limp-wristed, lesbians have short hair, etc. Stereotypes are often widely used to support bigoted attitudes and prejudice behavior.

Stonewall: The year was 1969, and this night of combat between mostly Black and Puerto Rican working-class drag queens and New York City cops opened the door to what is commonly known as the "Gay Rights Era." Throughout the early to mid 20th century, police raided gay bars across the country, and enacted unjustified violence on queers, particularly queers of color, nationwide. The raid on Stonewall was nothing new or surprising, nor was the fact that they fought back. But this night was the spark that revived a movement, and the participants went down in history as the revolutionaries responsible for securing the beginnings of gay civil rights.

Storm Scale: Michael Storm's Sexuality Scale further develops the Kinsey Scale by proposing a new chart that plots sexuality on an x-y axis in which bisexuality falls on the graphing area and hetero and homo on the x and y axe. This is an improvement on Kinsey's linear model because bisexuality does not fall in "between" two extremes, and this scale accounts for both behavior and fantasy. It does not, however, address transgenderism, transsexuality, or other queer identities.

Straight: Someone who is emotionally, spiritually, physically, and/or sexually attracted primarily to members of the "opposite" sex.

Transgender: An umbrella term for people whose *gender* identity is different from the *sex* and gender role they were assigned at birth. Transgender people do not necessarily want to have sex-reassignment surgery (SRS), but often "play" with gender or question gender roles. Transgender people can be heterosexual, homosexual, or bisexual and may or may not identify as queer. Sometimes called transgenderist (one who lives full-time as their preferred gender but does not get SRS), *Two-Spirit*, tranny, or TG.

Transsexual: I know this isn't in alphabetical order, but I thought it important to preface transphobia with definitions of *transsexual* and *transgender*. A transsexual is a person whose *gender* identity is different from the *sex* they were assigned at birth, so they take hormones or get sex reassignment surgery (SRS). There is an incredible range of reasons for taking this step. In many states after a period of time SRS recipients can legally change their name and other legal documents. Sometimes called *TS*.

Transphobia: Hatred and/or discrimination against people who break or blur *gender* roles and *sex* characteristics. Transphobia is mandated by a *gender regime* that says we are either man or woman, masculine or feminine. Like *biphobia*, it is prevalent in both straight and gay/lesbian communities. (See *oppression, prejudice, power*.)

Two-Spirit: The term *Two-Spirit* is a Native American concept present in some, but not all, indigenous cultures across North America and parts of Central and South America. It is a term of reverence, traditionally referring to people who display both masculine and feminine sex or gender characteristics. Named *berdache* by European colonists, those who are Two-Spirited are highly respected, and are often healers and leaders thought to possess a higher spiritual development. For more on this, see Colleen Donovan's interview with Qwo-Li Driskill, "Beginning Revolutions."

White supremacy: A historically based, institutionally perpetuated system of exploitation and oppression of continents, nations, and peoples of color by white people for the purpose of maintaining and defending a system of wealth, power, and privilege for whites. We live in a white-supremacist system in which white people are privileged at the expense of peoples of color. (See *racism, privilege, oppression, prejudice, power*.)

Ze: A pronoun used in place of she or he (terms used in a *binary* gender system) when you want to talk about someone whose gender doesn't neatly fit into a particular box. (See alsos *s/he*.)

plug in: resources for queer youth

Compiled with the help of the National Youth Advocacy Coalition

The National Youth Advocacy Coalition (NYAC) is dedicated to improving the lives of young people facing discrimination based on their sexual orientation. NYAC is the only national organization focused solely on improving the lives of gay, lesbian, bisexual, and transgender (GLBT) youth through advocacy, education, and information. NYAC advocates for and with GLBT youth through the collaboration of a broad spectrum of community-based and national organizations. Through this partnership, NYAC seeks to end discrimination against GLBT youth and to ensure their physical and emotional well-being.

Toll-Free Crisis and Peer Counseling Helplines

National Runaway Switchboard
800-621-4000
24 hours, 7 days

Trevor Helpline for Sexual Minority Youth
800-850-8078
24 hours, 7 days

Boston Alliance of Gay and Lesbian Youth
800-42-BAGLY (local only)
24 hours, 7 days

Out Youth
800-96-YOUTH
888-340-4528 (en español)
5:30 A.M. - 9:30 P.M., Central Time, 7 days

Indiana Youth Group
800-347-TEEN
7 P.M -10 P.M., Central Time, Fri.-Sat.

LYRIC Talkline
800-246-PRIDE (English and español, local only)
6:30 P.M.- 9:30 P.M., Pacific Time, Mon.-Sat.

The Gay & Lesbian National Hotline
888-THE-GLNH
6 P.M. - 10 P.M., EST, Mon.-Fri.
12 P.M. - 5 P.M., EST, Sat.

Inter/National Referral Services

These places will be able to help you find organizations and support groups for GLBTQ concerns in your area.

National Youth Advocacy Coalition
1711 Connecticut Avenue NW, Suite 206
Washington, DC 20009
202-319-7596
nyac@nyacyouth.org
http://www.nyacyouth.org

Gay, Lesbian, and Straight Education Network (GLSEN)
121 West 27th Street, Suite 804

New York, NY 10001
212-727-0135
http://www.glsen.org

International Gay and Lesbian Human Rights Commission
1360 Mission Street, Suite 200
San Francisco, CA 94103
415-255-8680
iglhrc@iglhrc.org
http://www.iglhrc.org

Intersex Society of North America (ISNA)
PO Box 3070
Ann Arbor, MI 48106-3070
info@isna.org
http://www.isna.org

Lesbian and Gay Immigration Rights Task Force
PO Box 7741
New York, NY 10116
212-818-9639
lgirtf@msn.com
http://www.lgirtf.org

National Black Lesbian and Gay Leadership Forum
1612 K Street NW, Suite 500
Washington, DC 20006
202-483-6786
http://www.nblglf.org

National Gay and Lesbian Task Force
2330 18th Street, NW

Washington, DC 20009
202-332-6483 ext. 3236
http://www.ngltf.org

National Latino/a Lesbian, Gay, Bisexual, and Transgendered Organization (LLEGO)
1612 K Street NW, Suite 500
Washington, DC 20006
888-633-8320
AquiLGBT@LLEGO.org
http://www.llego.org

Parents, Families, and Friends of Lesbians and Gays (PFLAG)
1101 14th Street NW, Suite 1030
Washington, DC 20005
202-638-4200
http://www.pflag.org

Student Pride (a project of GLSEN)
121 West 27th Street, Suite 804
New York, NY 10001
212-727-0135
http://www.studentprideUSA.org

Other Helpful Organizations

Asian & Pacific Islander, Queer & Questioning, Under 25, Altogether (AQUA)
730 Polk Street, 4th Floor
San Francisco, CA 94103

415-292-3400 ext. 362
aquakid@aquanet.org

Children of Lesbians and Gays Everywhere
3543 18th Street #17
San Francisco, CA 94110
415-861-5437
http://www.colage.org

FTM International
1360 Mission Street, Suite 200
San Francisco, CA 94103
415-553-5987
http://www.ftm-intl.org

Gender Political Advocacy Group (GenderPAC)
733 15th Street NW, 7th Floor
Washington, DC 20005
202-347-3024

Hetrick-Martin Institute for Lesbian and Gay Youth
2 Astor Place, Third Floor
New York, NY 10003
212-674-2400
212-674-8695 (TDD)

Lambda Legal Defense and Education Fund
120 Wall Street, Suite 1500
New York, NY 10005
212-809-8585

RAVE Youth Project
Gay and Lesbian Latino AIDS Education Initiative
1233 Locust St., 3rd Floor
Philadelphia, PA 19107
215-985-3382
http://www.critpath.org/galaei

San Francisco AIDS Foundation
995 Market St #200
San Francisco, CA 94103
415-487-3000
415-487-3004 (en español)
415-864-6606 (TDD)
http://www.sfaf.org

Sexual Minority Youth Assistance League (SMYAL)
410 7th Street SE
Washington, DC 20003
202-546-5940
http://www.smyal.org

Pen Pal Programs

Pen Pal Program—LA Center Youth Services
1625 North Shrader Blvd.
Los Angeles, CA 90028
23 and under, free newsletter

Pen Pal Scheme—International Lesbian and Gay Youth Organization
PO Box 542, NL-100 AM

Amsterdam, Netherlands
26 and under

Pen Pal Network
Indiana Youth Group
PO Box 20716
Indianapolis, IN 46220
21 and under

Lambda Youth Network
PO Box 7911
Culver City, CA 90233
23 and under

Rainbow Society
PO Box 6214
Santa Rosa, CA 95406
women only, all ages

Internet Resources

BlackTriangleGirl—for Sistahs of Color
http://www.blktriangurl.com/

Elight (for GLBT and questioning youth)
http://www.elight.org/

LGBT Youth of Color
http://www.youthresource.com/feat/poc/index.htm

Oasis (monthly online GLBT youth magazine)
http://www.oasismag.com

Outproud Online Group
http://www.outproud.org/

Planet Out (a community of LGBT people worldwide)
http://www.planetout.com

Queer America (directory of local and national GLBT groups)
http://www.queeramerica.com/

Queer Resources Directory
http://www.qrd.org/QRD/

Queer Youth Webring
http://www.youthresource.com/queeryouth/queeryouth.htm

Sistah Scape (for LBQ women of color)
http://www.sistahscape.com/

Youth Resource
http://www.youthresource.com

GLBT Religious Support Groups

Baptist: American Baptists Concerned
PO Box 16128
Oakland, CA 94610
510-530-6562

Buddhist: The San Francisco Zen Center
300 Page Street
San Francisco, CA 94102
415-863-3136

Episcopal: Integrity, Inc.
PO Box 5255
New York, NY 10185-5255
908-220-1914

Evangelical: Evangelicals Concerned
311 E. 72nd Street
Suite 1-G
New York, NY 10021
212-517-3171

Jewish: World Congress of Gay and Lesbian Jewish Organizations
PO Box 3345
New York, NY 10008-3345

MCC: Universal Fellowship of Metropolitan Community Churches
8704 Santa Monica Blvd., 2nd Floor
West Hollywood, CA 90069
310-360-8640

Mormon: Affirmation
PO Box 46022
Los Angeles, CA 90046
213-255-7251

Presbyterian: Presbyterians for Lesbian/Gay Concerns
PO Box 38
New Brunswick, NJ 08903-0038
908-249-1016

Quaker: Friends for Lesbian and Gay Concerns
143 Campbell Ave.
Ithaca, NY 14850
607-272-1024

Roman Catholic: Dignity/USA
1500 Massachusetts Avenue, NW , Suite 11
Washington, DC 20005
202-861-0017 or 800-877-8797

Unitarian Universalist: Unitarian Universalist Office of Lesbian, Bisexual, Gay, and Transgendered Concerns
25 Beacon Street
Boston, MA 02108
617-742-2100 ext. 470

about the editor

Amy Sonnie is a 24-year-old queer/feminist/writer/editor/activist. Committed to creating a forum for queer youth to speak out, she began working on this collection at 19, while attending Syracuse University. Originally from Pennsylvania, she now lives in San Francisco where she writes for various publications and recently cofounded RESYST, a queer youth art, education, and organizing project. This is her first book.